50 Pudding Dessert Recipes for Home

By: Kelly Johnson

Table of Contents

- Classic Cheeseburger
- Buffalo Chicken Wraps
- BBQ Pulled Pork Sandwiches
- Grilled Cheese and Tomato Soup
- Cobb Salad
- Chicken Caesar Salad
- Reuben Sandwich
- Philly Cheesesteak
- BLT Sandwich
- Sloppy Joes
- Chicken Fried Rice
- Meatball Sub
- Tuna Melt
- Chicken Quesadillas
- Southwest Chicken Salad
- Classic Club Sandwich
- French Dip Sandwich
- Fried Chicken Sandwich
- Turkey and Avocado Wrap
- Buffalo Chicken Wings
- Greek Salad with Chicken
- Spaghetti and Meatballs
- Fish Tacos
- Pork Tacos with Salsa Verde
- BBQ Chicken Pizza
- Veggie Burger
- Clubhouse Chicken Sandwich
- Lobster Roll
- Chicken Parmesan Sandwich
- Chili Con Carne
- Beef Stroganoff
- Chicken Tortilla Soup

- Southwest Beef Chili
- Tuna Salad Sandwich
- Asian Chicken Salad
- Crispy Chicken Tenders
- Beef Burritos
- Philly Cheesesteak Pizza
- Blackened Fish Sandwich
- Classic Macaroni and Cheese
- Chicken and Waffles
- Stuffed Bell Peppers
- Bacon and Egg Breakfast Sandwich
- Turkey Club Wrap
- Shrimp Po' Boy
- Spinach and Artichoke Dip
- BBQ Brisket Tacos
- Veggie Frittata
- Beef and Cheddar Sliders
- Roasted Vegetable Panini

Classic Cheeseburger

Ingredients:

- **Ground beef**: 1 lb (80% lean is ideal for juicy burgers)
- **Cheese**: 4 slices of cheddar or American cheese
- **Burger buns**: 4 (preferably toasted)
- **Lettuce**: 4 leaves
- **Tomato**: 1 large, sliced
- **Onion**: 1 small, sliced (red or yellow, depending on your preference)
- **Pickles**: 4-8 slices
- **Condiments**: Ketchup, mustard, and mayonnaise
- **Salt and pepper**: To taste
- **Optional**: Bacon strips, sautéed mushrooms, or other toppings you like

Instructions:

1. **Form the Patties**: Divide the ground beef into 4 equal portions and gently shape them into patties. Make a small indentation in the center of each patty with your thumb—this helps them cook evenly.
2. **Season**: Season both sides of each patty with salt and pepper just before cooking.
3. **Cook the Patties**:
    - **Grilling**: Preheat your grill to medium-high heat. Cook the patties for about 3-4 minutes on each side for medium-rare, or longer if you prefer them more well-done. Add the cheese slices during the last minute of cooking to let it melt.
    - **Pan-frying**: Heat a skillet over medium-high heat. Cook the patties for about 3-4 minutes on each side, adding the cheese during the last minute.
4. **Toast the Buns**: Place the buns on the grill or in a toaster while the patties are cooking, or use a skillet to toast them lightly.
5. **Assemble the Burgers**:
    - Spread your chosen condiments on the bottom half of each bun.
    - Place the cooked patty with melted cheese on top.
    - Add lettuce, tomato slices, onions, and pickles.
    - Top with the other half of the bun.
6. **Serve**: Serve immediately with your favorite sides, like fries or a salad.

Enjoy your classic cheeseburger!

Buffalo Chicken Wraps

Ingredients:

- **Chicken breasts**: 2 large, cooked and shredded (or use rotisserie chicken for convenience)
- **Buffalo sauce**: 1/2 cup (adjust to taste)
- **Ranch or blue cheese dressing**: 1/4 cup (plus extra for drizzling)
- **Shredded lettuce**: 1 cup
- **Cherry tomatoes**: 1/2 cup, halved
- **Shredded cheddar cheese**: 1/2 cup
- **Tortilla wraps**: 4 large
- **Optional**: Sliced avocado, sliced jalapeños, or diced celery for extra crunch

Instructions:

1. **Prepare the Chicken**:
   - If using raw chicken breasts, season them with salt and pepper, and cook them in a skillet over medium heat for 6-7 minutes per side, or until fully cooked. Alternatively, cook the chicken in the oven at 375°F (190°C) for 25-30 minutes.
   - Let the chicken cool slightly, then shred it with two forks or a hand mixer.
2. **Mix with Buffalo Sauce**: In a bowl, toss the shredded chicken with the buffalo sauce until well coated. Adjust the amount of sauce to your heat preference.
3. **Prepare the Wraps**: Lay out the tortillas on a flat surface. Spread a small amount of ranch or blue cheese dressing on each tortilla.
4. **Assemble the Wraps**:
   - Add a handful of shredded lettuce in the center of each tortilla.
   - Top with the buffalo chicken mixture.
   - Sprinkle with shredded cheddar cheese.
   - Add cherry tomatoes and any additional optional ingredients you like.
5. **Wrap and Serve**:
   - Fold in the sides of the tortilla and roll it up tightly from the bottom to the top.
   - If desired, you can grill the wraps in a skillet for 1-2 minutes on each side to get a crispy exterior and slightly melted cheese inside.
6. **Serve**: Slice the wraps in half diagonally and serve with extra ranch or blue cheese dressing for dipping.

Enjoy your spicy, tangy buffalo chicken wraps!

BBQ Pulled Pork Sandwiches

Ingredients:

For the Pulled Pork:

- **Pork shoulder (or pork butt)**: 4-5 lbs
- **BBQ rub**: 1/4 cup (store-bought or homemade; see below for a basic recipe)
- **Onion**: 1 large, sliced
- **Garlic**: 4 cloves, minced
- **Apple cider vinegar**: 1/2 cup
- **Chicken broth**: 1 cup
- **BBQ sauce**: 1 cup (your favorite kind)

For the Homemade BBQ Rub (optional):

- **Brown sugar**: 2 tbsp
- **Paprika**: 2 tbsp
- **Black pepper**: 1 tbsp
- **Salt**: 1 tbsp
- **Chili powder**: 1 tbsp
- **Cayenne pepper**: 1/2 tsp (optional, for heat)
- **Garlic powder**: 1 tsp
- **Onion powder**: 1 tsp

For Assembly:

- **Burger buns**: 4-6, preferably toasted
- **Coleslaw**: 2 cups (optional, for topping)
- **Pickles**: For garnish (optional)

Instructions:

1. **Prepare the Pork**:
    - **Apply the Rub**: Generously coat the pork shoulder with the BBQ rub. If you have time, let it sit for at least an hour, or overnight in the refrigerator for more flavor.
    - **Slow Cook**: Place the sliced onion and minced garlic in the bottom of a slow cooker. Add the pork shoulder on top. Pour the apple cider vinegar and chicken broth over the pork. Cook on low for 8-10 hours or on high for 4-5 hours, until the pork is tender and easily shreds.
2. **Shred the Pork**:
    - Remove the pork from the slow cooker and place it on a large cutting board or in a bowl. Shred the pork using two forks, discarding any large pieces of fat.
    - Return the shredded pork to the slow cooker and stir in the BBQ sauce. Let it cook for an additional 30 minutes on low to allow the flavors to meld.
3. **Assemble the Sandwiches**:
    - Toast the burger buns if desired.

- Pile the pulled pork onto the bottom half of each bun.
- Top with coleslaw and pickles if you like. Add the top half of the bun.
4. **Serve**: Serve the sandwiches warm with your favorite sides like potato salad, baked beans, or corn on the cob.

Tips:

- **Make Ahead**: The pulled pork can be made a day ahead and stored in the refrigerator. Reheat gently before serving.
- **Freezing**: Pulled pork freezes well. Store in an airtight container or freezer bag for up to 3 months. Thaw and reheat before serving.

Enjoy your delicious BBQ pulled pork sandwiches!

Grilled Cheese and Tomato Soup

Ingredients:

- **Bread**: 8 slices (preferably a sturdy type like sourdough, whole wheat, or classic white)
- **Cheese**: 8 slices (Cheddar, American, or a mix; you can also use shredded cheese)
- **Butter**: 4 tbsp (softened)

Instructions:

1. **Prepare the Bread**: Spread a thin layer of butter on one side of each slice of bread.
2. **Assemble the Sandwich**: Place a slice of cheese between two slices of bread, buttered sides facing out. If using shredded cheese, you can spread some on both slices of bread.
3. **Cook**: Heat a skillet over medium heat. Place the sandwiches in the skillet and cook for 2-4 minutes on each side, or until golden brown and the cheese is melted. Press down lightly with a spatula for even grilling.
4. **Serve**: Cut the sandwiches in half and serve hot.

Homemade Tomato Soup

Ingredients:

- **Olive oil**: 2 tbsp
- **Onion**: 1 large, chopped
- **Garlic**: 3 cloves, minced
- **Carrot**: 1 large, peeled and diced
- **Canned tomatoes**: 2 (14.5 oz) cans of diced tomatoes (or 4 cups of fresh tomatoes, peeled and chopped)
- **Chicken or vegetable broth**: 2 cups
- **Sugar**: 1 tsp (optional, to balance acidity)
- **Salt and pepper**: To taste
- **Dried basil**: 1 tsp (or 1 tbsp fresh basil, chopped)
- **Heavy cream or milk**: 1/2 cup (optional, for creaminess)
- **Croutons or fresh basil**: For garnish (optional)

Instructions:

1. **Sauté Vegetables**: Heat olive oil in a large pot over medium heat. Add the chopped onion, garlic, and carrot. Cook until the vegetables are softened, about 5-7 minutes.
2. **Add Tomatoes**: Stir in the canned tomatoes (with their juice) and the broth. Add sugar if using. Bring to a simmer and cook for 20 minutes, allowing the flavors to meld.
3. **Blend**: Use an immersion blender to blend the soup until smooth. Alternatively, carefully transfer the soup in batches to a blender. Return the soup to the pot after blending.

4. **Season**: Stir in the dried basil and season with salt and pepper to taste. If using, add the heavy cream or milk and heat through.
5. **Serve**: Ladle the soup into bowls and garnish with croutons or fresh basil if desired. Serve hot with the grilled cheese sandwiches.

Enjoy your classic combo of grilled cheese and tomato soup!

Cobb Salad

Ingredients:

- **Romaine lettuce**: 1 head, chopped
- **Cooked chicken**: 2 cups, diced (grilled or rotisserie chicken works well)
- **Bacon**: 6 slices, cooked and crumbled
- **Hard-boiled eggs**: 4, peeled and chopped
- **Avocado**: 1, peeled, pitted, and sliced
- **Tomatoes**: 1-2 large, diced (or use cherry tomatoes, halved)
- **Blue cheese**: 1/2 cup, crumbled (substitute with feta if preferred)
- **Red onion**: 1/4, finely chopped (optional)
- **Chives or green onions**: 2 tbsp, chopped (optional)

For the Dressing:

- **Olive oil**: 1/4 cup
- **Red wine vinegar**: 2 tbsp
- **Dijon mustard**: 1 tsp
- **Honey**: 1 tsp
- **Garlic**: 1 clove, minced
- **Salt and pepper**: To taste

Instructions:

1. **Prepare the Ingredients**:
   - Cook and crumble the bacon, and chop the cooked chicken.
   - Hard-boil the eggs, peel, and chop them.
   - Dice the tomatoes and slice the avocado.
   - If using, finely chop the red onion and chives or green onions.
2. **Make the Dressing**:
   - In a small bowl or jar, whisk together the olive oil, red wine vinegar, Dijon mustard, honey, minced garlic, salt, and pepper until well combined. Adjust seasoning to taste.
3. **Assemble the Salad**:
   - Arrange the chopped romaine lettuce on a large serving platter or individual plates.
   - Neatly arrange the chicken, bacon, eggs, avocado, tomatoes, blue cheese, and red onion (if using) in rows or sections over the lettuce.
4. **Serve**:
   - Drizzle with the dressing just before serving, or serve the dressing on the side so everyone can add their own.
   - Garnish with chopped chives or green onions if desired.

Tips:

- **Make Ahead**: You can prep the ingredients ahead of time and store them separately in the refrigerator. Assemble the salad just before serving to keep everything fresh.
- **Variations**: Feel free to add other ingredients like olives, bell peppers, or radishes based on your preferences.

Enjoy your delicious and satisfying Cobb salad!

Chicken Caesar Salad

Ingredients:

For the Salad:

- **Romaine lettuce**: 1 large head, chopped or torn into bite-sized pieces
- **Cooked chicken**: 2 cups, sliced or cubed (grilled or rotisserie chicken works well)
- **Croutons**: 1 cup (store-bought or homemade)
- **Parmesan cheese**: 1/2 cup, freshly grated or shaved
- **Cherry tomatoes**: 1 cup, halved (optional)
- **Red onion**: 1/4, thinly sliced (optional)

For the Caesar Dressing:

- **Mayonnaise**: 1/2 cup
- **Parmesan cheese**: 1/4 cup, grated
- **Garlic**: 2 cloves, minced
- **Lemon juice**: 2 tbsp (freshly squeezed)
- **Worcestershire sauce**: 1 tbsp
- **Dijon mustard**: 1 tsp
- **Salt and pepper**: To taste
- **Anchovy paste**: 1 tsp (optional, for traditional flavor)

Instructions:

1. **Prepare the Dressing:**
   - In a bowl, whisk together the mayonnaise, grated Parmesan cheese, minced garlic, lemon juice, Worcestershire sauce, Dijon mustard, and anchovy paste (if using). Season with salt and pepper to taste. Adjust seasoning as needed.
   - If you prefer a lighter dressing, you can substitute some or all of the mayonnaise with Greek yogurt.
2. **Prepare the Chicken:**
   - If you haven't already cooked the chicken, season it with salt and pepper, and grill or pan-sear until fully cooked. Let it rest for a few minutes before slicing or cubing.
3. **Prepare the Salad:**
   - In a large salad bowl, toss the chopped romaine lettuce with some of the Caesar dressing until lightly coated.
   - Add the sliced or cubed chicken on top of the lettuce.
   - Scatter croutons over the top, and sprinkle with freshly grated or shaved Parmesan cheese.
   - Add cherry tomatoes and red onion if using.
4. **Serve:**

- Serve immediately after assembling to ensure the croutons stay crisp. If desired, serve extra Caesar dressing on the side.

Tips:

- **Homemade Croutons**: To make your own croutons, toss cubed bread with olive oil, garlic powder, salt, and pepper, and bake at 375°F (190°C) for about 10-15 minutes, or until crispy.
- **Make-Ahead**: You can prepare the dressing and cook the chicken ahead of time. Store them separately and assemble the salad just before serving to keep the lettuce crisp.

Enjoy your delicious Chicken Caesar Salad!

Reuben Sandwich

Ingredients:

- **Rye bread**: 8 slices (preferably a good-quality rye)
- **Corned beef**: 1/2 lb, thinly sliced (deli-style or homemade)
- **Swiss cheese**: 4 slices
- **Sauerkraut**: 1 cup, drained well
- **Russian dressing or Thousand Island dressing**: 1/4 cup
- **Butter**: 4 tbsp (softened, for spreading on the bread)
- **Optional**: Pickles or additional mustard for serving

Instructions:

1. **Prepare the Ingredients**:
   - Drain the sauerkraut well to avoid soggy sandwiches. You can gently squeeze it in a clean towel or paper towels to remove excess moisture.
   - If using store-bought Russian or Thousand Island dressing, stir it well before using.
2. **Assemble the Sandwiches**:
   - Spread a thin layer of butter on one side of each slice of rye bread.
   - On the unbuttered side of four slices, spread a thin layer of Russian or Thousand Island dressing.
   - Layer the corned beef evenly over the dressing.
   - Top with the drained sauerkraut, followed by a slice of Swiss cheese.
   - Place the remaining slices of rye bread on top, buttered side out.
3. **Grill the Sandwiches**:
   - Heat a skillet or griddle over medium heat.
   - Place the assembled sandwiches in the skillet and cook for 3-4 minutes on each side, or until the bread is golden brown and the cheese is melted. Press down lightly with a spatula for even grilling.
4. **Serve**:
   - Remove the sandwiches from the skillet and let them sit for a minute before slicing in half. This helps to avoid cheese spilling out.
   - Serve with pickles and extra mustard or dressing on the side, if desired.

Tips:

- **Grilled to Perfection**: For an extra crispy texture, you can use a panini press or sandwich press if you have one.
- **Homemade Dressing**: If you want to make your own Russian or Thousand Island dressing, mix mayonnaise, ketchup, a splash of vinegar, a dash of hot sauce, and a bit of pickle relish.

Enjoy your classic Reuben sandwich!

Philly Cheesesteak

Ingredients:

- **Ribeye steak**: 1 lb, thinly sliced (or use a good-quality sirloin)
- **Onions**: 1 large, thinly sliced
- **Bell peppers**: 1-2, thinly sliced (optional, typically green bell pepper is used)
- **Provolone cheese**: 4-6 slices (or use Cheez Whiz for a traditional touch)
- **Hoagie rolls**: 4 (or sub with sub rolls or baguette-style bread)
- **Olive oil**: 2 tbsp
- **Salt and pepper**: To taste
- **Optional**: Mushrooms, sautéed (for added flavor)

Instructions:

1. **Prepare the Steak**:
   - Freeze the ribeye steak for about 1-2 hours to make it easier to slice thinly. Slice it against the grain into very thin strips.
   - Season the steak slices with salt and pepper.
2. **Cook the Vegetables**:
   - Heat 1 tablespoon of olive oil in a large skillet or griddle over medium heat.
   - Add the sliced onions (and bell peppers, if using). Cook until the onions are caramelized and the peppers are tender, about 10 minutes. Remove from the skillet and set aside.
3. **Cook the Steak**:
   - In the same skillet, add the remaining 1 tablespoon of olive oil.
   - Add the thinly sliced steak in a single layer (you may need to do this in batches). Cook for 2-3 minutes on each side until just browned and cooked through. Avoid overcooking to keep the steak tender.
4. **Combine Steak and Vegetables**:
   - Add the cooked onions and peppers back into the skillet with the steak. Mix everything together.
5. **Add Cheese**:
   - Lower the heat and layer the provolone cheese slices over the steak and vegetable mixture. Cover the skillet with a lid to help the cheese melt. If using Cheez Whiz, you can add it directly on the steak or warm it separately and drizzle over the sandwich.
6. **Prepare the Rolls**:
   - While the cheese is melting, split the hoagie rolls but don't cut all the way through. You can toast them lightly in the oven or on a skillet if desired.
7. **Assemble the Sandwiches**:
   - Divide the steak and cheese mixture among the hoagie rolls, spooning it generously into each roll.

8. **Serve**:
   - Serve immediately while the cheese is gooey and the bread is warm.

Tips:

- **Beef**: For an authentic texture, using ribeye steak is preferred due to its marbling and flavor. If thinly sliced ribeye isn't available, look for pre-sliced steak or have your butcher slice it for you.
- **Cheese**: Provolone is classic, but if you want an extra cheesy experience, you can mix in some Cheez Whiz or American cheese.
- **Toppings**: Feel free to customize with additional toppings like mushrooms, hot peppers, or even a spread of mayonnaise or mustard.

Enjoy your homemade Philly Cheesesteak!

BLT Sandwich

Ingredients:

- **Bacon**: 6-8 slices
- **Lettuce**: 4-6 leaves (romaine or iceberg works well)
- **Tomato**: 1 large, sliced (preferably vine-ripened or heirloom)
- **Bread**: 4 slices (white, whole wheat, or sourdough; preferably toasted)
- **Mayonnaise**: 1/4 cup (or to taste)
- **Salt and pepper**: To taste

Instructions:

1. **Cook the Bacon**:
    - **Skillet Method**: Heat a skillet over medium heat. Add the bacon slices in a single layer and cook until crispy, about 6-8 minutes, turning occasionally. Drain on paper towels.
    - **Oven Method**: Preheat the oven to 400°F (200°C). Arrange the bacon slices on a baking sheet lined with parchment paper or a rack. Bake for 15-20 minutes, or until crispy. Drain on paper towels.
2. **Prepare the Bread**:
    - Toast the bread slices to your desired level of crispiness.
3. **Prepare the Vegetables**:
    - Wash and pat dry the lettuce leaves.
    - Slice the tomato into thick, even slices. Season with a little salt and pepper if desired.
4. **Assemble the Sandwiches**:
    - Spread mayonnaise evenly on one side of each slice of toasted bread.
    - On the mayo-coated side of one slice, layer the lettuce leaves.
    - Add the tomato slices on top of the lettuce.
    - Place the crispy bacon slices over the tomato.
    - Top with the remaining slice of bread, mayo side down.
5. **Serve**:
    - Cut the sandwich in half diagonally for easy eating, and serve immediately.

Tips:

- **Bacon**: For extra flavor, you can season the bacon with a little black pepper or brown sugar before cooking.
- **Bread**: Toasting the bread adds crunch and helps prevent the sandwich from becoming soggy.
- **Variations**: Add avocado slices or a slice of cheese for a twist on the classic BLT.

Enjoy your perfect BLT sandwich!

Sloppy Joes

Ingredients:

- **Ground beef**: 1 lb (you can also use ground turkey or chicken)
- **Onion**: 1 medium, finely chopped
- **Green bell pepper**: 1/2, finely chopped (optional)
- **Garlic**: 2 cloves, minced
- **Tomato sauce**: 1 cup
- **Ketchup**: 1/4 cup
- **Worcestershire sauce**: 2 tbsp
- **Brown sugar**: 1 tbsp
- **Mustard**: 1 tbsp (yellow or Dijon)
- **Apple cider vinegar**: 1 tbsp
- **Salt and pepper**: To taste
- **Red pepper flakes**: 1/4 tsp (optional, for a little heat)
- **Hamburger buns**: 4-6, toasted if desired

Instructions:

1. **Cook the Beef**:
   - In a large skillet over medium heat, cook the ground beef until browned, breaking it up with a spoon as it cooks. Drain excess fat if necessary.
2. **Add Vegetables**:
   - Add the chopped onion (and green bell pepper if using) to the skillet. Cook for 5-7 minutes, or until the onion is softened.
   - Stir in the minced garlic and cook for an additional 1-2 minutes.
3. **Add the Sauce Ingredients**:
   - Stir in the tomato sauce, ketchup, Worcestershire sauce, brown sugar, mustard, apple cider vinegar, salt, pepper, and red pepper flakes if using.
   - Bring the mixture to a simmer and cook for 10-15 minutes, stirring occasionally, until the sauce has thickened and the flavors are well combined.
4. **Serve**:
   - Spoon the Sloppy Joe mixture onto the bottom half of the hamburger buns.
   - Top with the other half of the bun and serve immediately.

Tips:

- **Consistency**: If the mixture is too thick, you can add a bit of water or beef broth to reach your desired consistency.
- **Make Ahead**: The Sloppy Joe mixture can be made ahead of time and stored in the refrigerator for up to 3 days. Reheat before serving.

- **Freezing**: You can freeze the Sloppy Joe mixture for up to 3 months. Thaw in the refrigerator overnight before reheating.

Enjoy your hearty, flavorful Sloppy Joes!

Chicken Fried Rice

Ingredients:

- **Cooked chicken**: 2 cups, diced or shredded (use leftover or rotisserie chicken)
- **Rice**: 3 cups, cooked and cooled (best if you use day-old rice for better texture)
- **Vegetable oil**: 2 tbsp
- **Onion**: 1 small, diced
- **Garlic**: 2 cloves, minced
- **Carrots**: 1/2 cup, diced
- **Frozen peas**: 1/2 cup
- **Eggs**: 2, lightly beaten
- **Soy sauce**: 3 tbsp
- **Oyster sauce**: 1 tbsp (optional)
- **Sesame oil**: 1 tsp (optional)
- **Green onions**: 2-3, sliced
- **Salt and pepper**: To taste

Instructions:

1. **Prepare the Ingredients**:
    - Make sure the rice is cooked and cooled. Day-old rice works best as it's less likely to be mushy.
    - Dice or shred the cooked chicken into bite-sized pieces.
    - Dice the onion and carrots. Mince the garlic. Slice the green onions.
2. **Cook the Vegetables**:
    - Heat the vegetable oil in a large skillet or wok over medium-high heat.
    - Add the diced onion and cook for 2-3 minutes until translucent.
    - Add the garlic and diced carrots. Cook for another 2-3 minutes until the carrots are tender.
3. **Add the Chicken and Rice**:
    - Add the diced chicken to the skillet and stir to combine.
    - Push the chicken and vegetables to one side of the skillet. Add a little more oil if needed and add the cooked rice to the empty side of the skillet.
    - Stir-fry the rice for a few minutes until heated through and starting to crisp up. Mix the rice with the chicken and vegetables.
4. **Add the Eggs**:
    - Push the rice mixture to one side of the skillet again. Pour the beaten eggs into the empty side of the skillet.
    - Scramble the eggs until fully cooked, then mix them into the rice and chicken.
5. **Season and Finish**:
    - Add soy sauce, oyster sauce (if using), and sesame oil. Stir to coat everything evenly.

- Add frozen peas and cook for another 2-3 minutes until they are heated through.
- Season with salt and pepper to taste. Stir in the sliced green onions just before serving.
6. **Serve**:
    - Serve the Chicken Fried Rice hot, straight from the skillet.

Tips:

- **Rice**: For the best texture, use rice that has been cooked and cooled, ideally overnight. This helps prevent the rice from becoming mushy.
- **Vegetables**: Feel free to customize with additional vegetables like bell peppers, corn, or broccoli.
- **Sauce**: Adjust the amount of soy sauce to your taste. For a less salty option, use low-sodium soy sauce.

Enjoy your homemade Chicken Fried Rice!

Meatball Sub

Ingredients:

For the Meatballs:

- **Ground beef**: 1 lb (you can also use a mix of beef and pork)
- **Breadcrumbs**: 1/2 cup (Italian seasoned or plain)
- **Parmesan cheese**: 1/4 cup, grated
- **Egg**: 1, beaten
- **Garlic**: 2 cloves, minced
- **Parsley**: 2 tbsp, chopped (fresh or 1 tbsp dried)
- **Salt and pepper**: To taste
- **Olive oil**: For frying or baking

For the Subs:

- **Marinara sauce**: 2 cups (store-bought or homemade)
- **Sub rolls**: 4 (or hoagie rolls)
- **Mozzarella cheese**: 1 cup, shredded (or sliced provolone)
- **Optional**: Fresh basil or extra Parmesan cheese for garnish

Instructions:

1. **Prepare the Meatballs**:
   - Preheat your oven to 375°F (190°C) if you plan to bake the meatballs.
   - In a large bowl, combine the ground beef, breadcrumbs, Parmesan cheese, beaten egg, minced garlic, chopped parsley, salt, and pepper. Mix until well combined, but don't overmix.
   - Shape the mixture into 1-inch meatballs and place them on a baking sheet lined with parchment paper or a lightly greased baking dish.
   - **To Bake**: Bake in the preheated oven for 20-25 minutes, or until the meatballs are cooked through and browned.
   - **To Fry**: Heat a little olive oil in a skillet over medium heat. Fry the meatballs in batches, turning occasionally, until browned and cooked through, about 10-12 minutes.
2. **Heat the Marinara Sauce**:
   - While the meatballs are cooking, heat the marinara sauce in a saucepan over medium heat until warmed through.
3. **Assemble the Subs**:
   - Slice the sub rolls lengthwise, but don't cut all the way through. If you like, you can lightly toast the rolls in the oven or on a skillet.
   - Spoon some marinara sauce onto the bottom of each roll.
   - Place 3-4 meatballs in each roll, depending on their size.

- Pour additional marinara sauce over the meatballs.
- Sprinkle or layer shredded mozzarella cheese (or provolone) on top.

4. **Melt the Cheese**:
   - If the rolls are not toasted, place the assembled subs under a broiler for 1-2 minutes, or until the cheese is melted and bubbly. Keep a close eye to avoid burning.
   - Alternatively, you can place the subs in a preheated oven at 375°F (190°C) for about 5-7 minutes to melt the cheese.

5. **Serve**:
   - Garnish with fresh basil or extra Parmesan cheese if desired.
   - Serve the Meatball Subs hot and enjoy!

Tips:

- **Meatball Size**: Make sure meatballs are uniform in size for even cooking.
- **Sauce**: If you prefer a spicier or more seasoned sauce, you can add red pepper flakes, Italian seasoning, or extra garlic to the marinara.
- **Customization**: Feel free to add sautéed peppers or onions for extra flavor.

Enjoy your homemade Meatball Subs!

Tuna Melt

Ingredients:

For the Tuna Salad:

- **Canned tuna**: 1 can (5-6 oz), drained
- **Mayonnaise**: 1/4 cup
- **Celery**: 1 stalk, finely chopped
- **Red onion**: 1/4, finely chopped
- **Pickles**: 2 tbsp, finely chopped (optional)
- **Dijon mustard**: 1 tsp (optional)
- **Lemon juice**: 1 tsp
- **Salt and pepper**: To taste
- **Fresh parsley or dill**: 1 tbsp, chopped (optional)

For the Sandwich:

- **Bread**: 4 slices (rye, sourdough, or whole wheat are good choices)
- **Cheese**: 4 slices (Swiss, cheddar, or American work well)
- **Butter**: 2 tbsp (softened, for spreading on the bread)

Instructions:

1. **Prepare the Tuna Salad**:
    - In a bowl, combine the drained tuna, mayonnaise, finely chopped celery, red onion, pickles (if using), Dijon mustard, and lemon juice. Mix well.
    - Season with salt and pepper to taste. Stir in chopped parsley or dill if desired.
2. **Assemble the Sandwiches**:
    - Spread a thin layer of butter on one side of each slice of bread.
    - On the unbuttered side of two slices, spread a generous amount of the tuna salad.
    - Place a slice of cheese on top of the tuna salad.
    - Top with the remaining slices of bread, buttered side facing out.
3. **Grill the Sandwiches**:
    - Heat a skillet or griddle over medium heat.
    - Place the sandwiches in the skillet and cook for 3-4 minutes on each side, or until the bread is golden brown and the cheese is melted. Press down slightly with a spatula to ensure even grilling.
4. **Serve**:
    - Remove the sandwiches from the skillet and let them cool for a minute before cutting in half.
    - Serve hot.

Tips:

- **Cheese**: For an extra cheesy melt, you can use a mix of cheeses or add extra slices.
- **Bread**: For a crispier texture, you can toast the bread lightly before assembling the sandwich.
- **Additions**: Customize your Tuna Melt with add-ins like sliced tomatoes, lettuce, or even a slice of bacon for extra flavor.

Enjoy your classic and comforting Tuna Melt!

Chicken Quesadillas

Ingredients:

For the Chicken Filling:

- **Cooked chicken**: 2 cups, shredded or diced (rotisserie or leftover chicken works well)
- **Olive oil**: 1 tbsp
- **Onion**: 1 small, finely chopped
- **Bell pepper**: 1, finely chopped (any color)
- **Garlic**: 2 cloves, minced
- **Ground cumin**: 1 tsp
- **Chili powder**: 1 tsp
- **Paprika**: 1/2 tsp
- **Salt and pepper**: To taste

For the Quesadillas:

- **Flour tortillas**: 4 large (8-inch or 10-inch)
- **Cheese**: 2 cups, shredded (cheddar, Monterey Jack, or a Mexican blend)
- **Butter**: 2 tbsp (softened, for spreading on the tortillas)

Optional Add-ins:

- **Fresh cilantro**: 2 tbsp, chopped
- **Jalapeños**: 1, sliced (for a bit of heat)
- **Salsa**: For serving
- **Sour cream**: For serving
- **Guacamole**: For serving

Instructions:

1. **Prepare the Chicken Filling**:
    - Heat olive oil in a skillet over medium heat.
    - Add the chopped onion and bell pepper. Cook for 5-7 minutes, or until the vegetables are softened.
    - Add the minced garlic, ground cumin, chili powder, paprika, salt, and pepper. Cook for another 1-2 minutes, stirring frequently.
    - Stir in the shredded or diced chicken and cook until heated through. Adjust seasoning if needed.
2. **Assemble the Quesadillas**:
    - Spread a thin layer of softened butter on one side of each tortilla.
    - Place a tortilla, buttered side down, in a large skillet over medium heat.
    - Sprinkle a layer of shredded cheese evenly over the tortilla.

- Spoon some of the chicken mixture over the cheese.
- Sprinkle a bit more cheese on top of the chicken to help it melt and hold everything together.
- Place another tortilla on top, buttered side up.

3. **Cook the Quesadillas**:
   - Cook for 3-4 minutes on each side, or until the tortillas are golden brown and crispy and the cheese is melted. You may need to adjust the heat to avoid burning the tortillas.
   - Use a large spatula to flip the quesadilla carefully.

4. **Serve**:
   - Remove from the skillet and let cool for a minute before cutting into wedges.
   - Serve with salsa, sour cream, and guacamole if desired.

Tips:

- **Cheese**: A good melting cheese is key. Monterey Jack and cheddar are great choices. You can also use a Mexican cheese blend.
- **Customization**: Feel free to add other fillings like black beans, corn, or sliced olives.
- **Make-Ahead**: The chicken filling can be made ahead of time and stored in the refrigerator for up to 3 days. Just assemble and cook the quesadillas when ready to serve.

Enjoy your tasty and satisfying Chicken Quesadillas!

Southwest Chicken Salad

Ingredients:

For the Salad:

- **Cooked chicken**: 2 cups, grilled or baked, and sliced or diced (use seasoned chicken for extra flavor)
- **Romaine lettuce**: 4 cups, chopped
- **Black beans**: 1 can (15 oz), drained and rinsed
- **Corn**: 1 cup (fresh, frozen, or canned)
- **Cherry tomatoes**: 1 cup, halved
- **Red bell pepper**: 1, diced
- **Avocado**: 1, diced
- **Red onion**: 1/4, thinly sliced
- **Cilantro**: 2 tbsp, chopped (optional)
- **Cheddar cheese**: 1/2 cup, shredded
- **Tortilla strips**: 1/2 cup (store-bought or homemade)

For the Southwest Dressing:

- **Greek yogurt**: 1/2 cup
- **Mayonnaise**: 1/4 cup
- **Lime juice**: 2 tbsp (freshly squeezed)
- **Honey**: 1 tbsp
- **Chili powder**: 1/2 tsp
- **Cumin**: 1/2 tsp
- **Garlic powder**: 1/2 tsp
- **Salt and pepper**: To taste

Instructions:

1. **Prepare the Chicken**:
   - Season the chicken with your favorite spices or a Southwest seasoning blend. Grill or bake until fully cooked. Allow it to rest for a few minutes before slicing or dicing.
2. **Cook the Corn**:
   - If using fresh or frozen corn, cook it according to package instructions or until tender. If using canned corn, simply drain it.
3. **Prepare the Dressing**:
   - In a small bowl, whisk together Greek yogurt, mayonnaise, lime juice, honey, chili powder, cumin, garlic powder, salt, and pepper. Adjust seasoning to taste. Refrigerate until ready to use.
4. **Assemble the Salad**:

- In a large salad bowl, combine the chopped romaine lettuce, black beans, corn, cherry tomatoes, diced red bell pepper, avocado, and sliced red onion.
- Add the cooked chicken on top of the salad mixture.
- Sprinkle with shredded cheddar cheese and tortilla strips.
- Garnish with chopped cilantro if desired.
5. **Serve**:
    - Serve the salad with the Southwest dressing on the side or drizzled on top just before serving.

Tips:

- **Chicken**: For a more intense flavor, marinate the chicken in a mix of lime juice, olive oil, and Southwest spices before cooking.
- **Tortilla Strips**: To make homemade tortilla strips, cut tortillas into strips, toss with a little oil, and bake at 400°F (200°C) for 5-7 minutes, or until crispy.
- **Additions**: Feel free to add extras like sliced jalapeños, diced green onions, or black olives for more flavor.

Enjoy your fresh and flavorful Southwest Chicken Salad!

Classic Club Sandwich

Ingredients:

- **Bread**: 3 slices per sandwich (white, whole wheat, or sourdough)
- **Turkey**: 4-6 slices (deli turkey or cooked turkey breast)
- **Bacon**: 4 slices, cooked until crispy
- **Lettuce**: 2-3 leaves (iceberg or romaine)
- **Tomato**: 1 large, sliced
- **Mayonnaise**: 2-3 tbsp
- **Salt and pepper**: To taste

Instructions:

1. **Toast the Bread**:
    - Toast the 3 slices of bread per sandwich until golden brown and crispy.
2. **Prepare the Ingredients**:
    - Cook the bacon until crispy and drain on paper towels.
    - Wash and dry the lettuce leaves.
    - Slice the tomato into thick, even slices.
3. **Assemble the Sandwich**:
    - Spread a layer of mayonnaise on one side of each slice of toasted bread.
    - On the first slice of bread, layer turkey slices, followed by a few bacon strips, and then a layer of lettuce and tomato. Season with a pinch of salt and pepper if desired.
    - Top with the second slice of bread, mayonnaise side down.
    - Spread mayonnaise on the top side of the second slice of bread.
    - Add another layer of turkey, bacon, lettuce, and tomato.
    - Place the third slice of bread on top, mayonnaise side down.
4. **Slice and Serve**:
    - Carefully cut the sandwich into quarters or halves, securing each section with toothpicks if needed to keep everything together.
    - Serve immediately with your choice of side (chips, pickles, or a simple salad).

Tips:

- **Variations**: You can add extras like avocado slices, cheese (Swiss, cheddar, or American), or replace turkey with chicken or ham.
- **Bread**: For added flavor, consider using a rustic bread or even a lightly buttered and grilled bread.
- **Presentation**: For a professional touch, you can also garnish with a few extra pickles or olives on the side.

Enjoy your classic and satisfying Club Sandwich!

French Dip Sandwich

Ingredients:

For the Sandwich:

- **Beef**: 1 lb (such as roast beef or thinly sliced deli beef)
- **Sub rolls**: 4 (or hoagie rolls, baguettes, or other crusty rolls)
- **Swiss cheese**: 4 slices (or provolone)
- **Butter**: 2 tbsp (softened, for spreading on the bread)

For the Au Jus:

- **Beef broth**: 2 cups
- **Onion**: 1 small, finely chopped
- **Garlic**: 2 cloves, minced
- **Worcestershire sauce**: 1 tbsp
- **Soy sauce**: 1 tbsp
- **Dried thyme**: 1/2 tsp
- **Salt and pepper**: To taste

Instructions:

1. **Prepare the Au Jus:**
   - In a medium saucepan, heat a little oil over medium heat.
   - Add the finely chopped onion and cook until softened, about 5 minutes.
   - Add the minced garlic and cook for an additional minute.
   - Pour in the beef broth, Worcestershire sauce, soy sauce, and dried thyme.
   - Bring to a simmer and cook for about 10-15 minutes, allowing the flavors to meld. Adjust seasoning with salt and pepper as needed. Keep warm.
2. **Prepare the Beef:**
   - If using pre-cooked roast beef, thinly slice it against the grain.
   - If using deli roast beef, it's usually ready to use. Warm it gently in the microwave or a skillet if desired.
3. **Toast the Rolls:**
   - Preheat your oven to 375°F (190°C).
   - Spread a thin layer of softened butter on the cut sides of the rolls.
   - Place the rolls on a baking sheet and toast in the oven for about 5 minutes, or until lightly golden and crisp.
4. **Assemble the Sandwiches:**
   - Layer the sliced roast beef evenly on the bottom half of each toasted roll.
   - Place a slice of Swiss cheese on top of the beef.
   - Return the assembled sandwiches to the oven for a few minutes, just long enough for the cheese to melt.

5. **Serve:**
    - Remove the sandwiches from the oven.
    - Serve hot with the au jus on the side for dipping.

Tips:

- **Beef**: For extra flavor, you can use leftover roast beef or cook a small beef roast and slice it thinly.
- **Bread**: Choose crusty rolls or baguettes that will hold up well to dipping.
- **Au Jus Variations**: For added depth of flavor, you can add a splash of red wine or a bit of balsamic vinegar to the au jus.

Enjoy your delicious and comforting French Dip Sandwich!

Fried Chicken Sandwich

Ingredients:

For the Chicken:

- **Chicken breasts**: 2 large, boneless and skinless
- **Buttermilk**: 1 cup (for marinating)
- **All-purpose flour**: 1 cup
- **Cornstarch**: 1/4 cup
- **Paprika**: 1 tsp
- **Garlic powder**: 1 tsp
- **Onion powder**: 1 tsp
- **Cayenne pepper**: 1/2 tsp (optional, for heat)
- **Salt**: 1 tsp
- **Black pepper**: 1/2 tsp
- **Eggs**: 2, beaten
- **Vegetable oil**: For frying

For the Sandwich:

- **Brioche buns**: 4 (or other sandwich rolls)
- **Mayonnaise**: 1/4 cup
- **Pickles**: 8-10 slices (dill or bread-and-butter)
- **Shredded lettuce**: 1 cup
- **Tomato**: 1 large, sliced (optional)

Instructions:

1. **Marinate the Chicken**:
    - Place the chicken breasts in a bowl and cover with buttermilk. Marinate in the refrigerator for at least 1 hour, or overnight for best results.
2. **Prepare the Breading**:
    - In a large bowl, mix together the flour, cornstarch, paprika, garlic powder, onion powder, cayenne pepper (if using), salt, and black pepper.
    - In another bowl, beat the eggs.
3. **Bread the Chicken**:
    - Remove the chicken breasts from the buttermilk, allowing excess to drip off.
    - Dip the chicken into the beaten eggs, then dredge thoroughly in the flour mixture, pressing gently to adhere.
4. **Fry the Chicken**:
    - Heat vegetable oil in a large skillet or deep fryer to 350°F (175°C). You need enough oil to submerge the chicken or at least cover half of it.

- Fry the chicken breasts in batches, if necessary, for 5-7 minutes per side, or until the internal temperature reaches 165°F (74°C) and the breading is golden brown and crispy.
- Remove the chicken from the oil and drain on a wire rack or paper towels.

5. **Assemble the Sandwiches**:
    - Toast the brioche buns lightly, if desired.
    - Spread mayonnaise on the bottom half of each bun.
    - Place a fried chicken breast on the bun.
    - Top with pickles, shredded lettuce, and tomato slices (if using).
    - Place the top half of the bun on the sandwich.
6. **Serve**:
    - Serve the sandwiches hot with your favorite side dishes, such as fries or coleslaw.

Tips:

- **Buttermilk Marinade**: Marinating in buttermilk helps tenderize the chicken and adds flavor.
- **Crispy Coating**: For extra crispy coating, you can double dip the chicken (buttermilk, then flour mixture, then buttermilk, and flour mixture again).
- **Oil Temperature**: Maintain the oil temperature to ensure even cooking and prevent sogginess. Use a thermometer to monitor the temperature.

Enjoy your homemade Fried Chicken Sandwich!

Turkey and Avocado Wrap

Ingredients:

- **Tortillas**: 4 large (flour or whole wheat)
- **Turkey**: 8 oz (deli slices or cooked turkey breast, thinly sliced)
- **Avocado**: 1 ripe, sliced
- **Lettuce**: 1 cup (shredded or whole leaves, such as romaine or iceberg)
- **Tomato**: 1 large, sliced
- **Cucumber**: 1/2, thinly sliced (optional)
- **Red onion**: 1/4, thinly sliced (optional)
- **Cheese**: 4 slices (Swiss, cheddar, or your favorite cheese)
- **Mayonnaise**: 2 tbsp (or use mustard, hummus, or your preferred spread)
- **Salt and pepper**: To taste

Instructions:

1. **Prepare the Ingredients**:
    - Slice the avocado, tomato, cucumber, and red onion if using.
    - Shred or slice the lettuce if not using pre-shredded.
2. **Prepare the Wraps**:
    - Spread a thin layer of mayonnaise (or your chosen spread) evenly over one side of each tortilla.
    - Lay a slice of cheese in the center of each tortilla.
3. **Assemble the Wraps**:
    - Place a layer of turkey slices on top of the cheese.
    - Arrange the avocado slices over the turkey.
    - Add the lettuce, tomato slices, cucumber, and red onion (if using).
    - Season with a pinch of salt and pepper to taste.
4. **Wrap It Up**:
    - Fold the sides of the tortilla in towards the center, then roll up from the bottom to enclose the fillings. Ensure it's tightly wrapped.
5. **Serve**:
    - Cut the wraps in half on a diagonal if desired, and serve immediately.

Tips:

- **Customization**: Feel free to add extras like shredded carrots, bell peppers, or sprouts for additional crunch and flavor.
- **Avocado**: To prevent the avocado from browning, you can drizzle a little lemon or lime juice on it.
- **Tortilla**: Warm the tortilla in a dry skillet for a few seconds on each side to make it more pliable, which makes wrapping easier.

Enjoy your tasty and refreshing Turkey and Avocado Wrap!

Buffalo Chicken Wings

Ingredients:

For the Chicken Wings:

- **Chicken wings**: 2 lbs (split into flats and drumettes, if needed)
- **Baking powder**: 1 tbsp (helps with crispiness, not baking powder)
- **Salt**: 1 tsp
- **Black pepper**: 1/2 tsp
- **Garlic powder**: 1/2 tsp
- **Onion powder**: 1/2 tsp
- **Paprika**: 1/2 tsp (optional, for color and flavor)

For the Buffalo Sauce:

- **Hot sauce**: 1/2 cup (Frank's RedHot is a classic choice)
- **Unsalted butter**: 1/4 cup (1/2 stick)
- **Garlic powder**: 1/2 tsp
- **Worcestershire sauce**: 1 tbsp
- **Honey**: 1 tbsp (optional, for a touch of sweetness)
- **Salt**: To taste

For Serving:

- **Celery sticks**: 1 bunch, cut into sticks
- **Carrot sticks**: 1 bunch, cut into sticks
- **Ranch dressing or blue cheese dressing**: For dipping

Instructions:

1. **Prepare the Chicken Wings**:
    - Preheat your oven to 425°F (220°C).
    - Pat the chicken wings dry with paper towels. This step is crucial for getting them crispy.
    - In a large bowl, toss the wings with baking powder, salt, black pepper, garlic powder, onion powder, and paprika until evenly coated.
2. **Bake the Wings**:
    - Arrange the wings in a single layer on a wire rack set over a baking sheet. The wire rack helps the heat circulate around the wings, making them crispier.
    - Bake in the preheated oven for 40-45 minutes, or until the wings are golden brown and crispy, flipping them halfway through.
3. **Prepare the Buffalo Sauce**:

- While the wings are baking, melt the butter in a small saucepan over medium heat.
- Stir in the hot sauce, garlic powder, Worcestershire sauce, and honey (if using). Simmer for 2-3 minutes, then remove from heat. Adjust seasoning with salt if needed.

4. **Toss the Wings**:
   - Once the wings are done baking, transfer them to a large bowl.
   - Pour the Buffalo sauce over the wings and toss until they are evenly coated.
5. **Serve**:
   - Arrange the wings on a serving platter.
   - Serve with celery and carrot sticks, and your choice of ranch or blue cheese dressing for dipping.

Tips:

- **Frying Option**: If you prefer fried wings, heat oil in a deep fryer or large pot to 375°F (190°C) and fry the wings in batches for about 8-10 minutes, or until crispy and cooked through. Then toss in the sauce as directed.
- **Spice Level**: Adjust the amount of hot sauce or add cayenne pepper if you like your wings extra spicy.
- **Make-Ahead**: You can prepare the wings and sauce ahead of time. Reheat the wings in the oven before tossing them in the sauce for a fresh-out-of-the-oven taste.

Enjoy your delicious and spicy Buffalo Chicken Wings!

Greek Salad with Chicken

Ingredients:

For the Salad:

- **Chicken breasts**: 2, boneless and skinless
- **Olive oil**: 2 tbsp (for grilling the chicken)
- **Lemon juice**: 1 tbsp (for marinating the chicken)
- **Garlic**: 2 cloves, minced (for marinating the chicken)
- **Dried oregano**: 1 tsp (for marinating the chicken)
- **Salt and pepper**: To taste
- **Roma tomatoes**: 2, chopped
- **Cucumber**: 1 large, diced
- **Red onion**: 1/4, thinly sliced
- **Kalamata olives**: 1/2 cup, pitted
- **Feta cheese**: 1/2 cup, crumbled
- **Fresh parsley**: 2 tbsp, chopped (optional)

For the Dressing:

- **Olive oil**: 1/4 cup
- **Lemon juice**: 2 tbsp (freshly squeezed)
- **Red wine vinegar**: 1 tbsp
- **Dijon mustard**: 1 tsp
- **Garlic**: 1 clove, minced
- **Dried oregano**: 1/2 tsp
- **Salt and pepper**: To taste

Instructions:

1. **Marinate and Grill the Chicken:**
    - In a bowl, mix together olive oil, lemon juice, minced garlic, dried oregano, salt, and pepper.
    - Add the chicken breasts to the marinade, making sure they are well-coated. Let them marinate for at least 30 minutes, or up to 2 hours in the refrigerator.
    - Preheat the grill or a grill pan over medium-high heat.
    - Grill the chicken for 6-7 minutes per side, or until fully cooked and the internal temperature reaches 165°F (74°C). Allow the chicken to rest for a few minutes before slicing it into strips.
2. **Prepare the Salad:**
    - In a large bowl, combine chopped tomatoes, diced cucumber, thinly sliced red onion, Kalamata olives, and crumbled feta cheese.
    - Optionally, add chopped fresh parsley for extra flavor and color.

3. **Make the Dressing:**
   - In a small bowl, whisk together olive oil, lemon juice, red wine vinegar, Dijon mustard, minced garlic, dried oregano, salt, and pepper until well combined.
4. **Assemble the Salad:**
   - Add the grilled chicken strips to the salad bowl.
   - Drizzle the dressing over the salad and toss gently to combine all the ingredients.
5. **Serve:**
   - Serve the Greek Salad with Chicken immediately, or chill in the refrigerator for 30 minutes if you prefer a colder salad.

Tips:

- **Chicken Variation**: For a quicker option, you can use pre-cooked chicken or rotisserie chicken.
- **Vegetable Options**: Feel free to add other vegetables like bell peppers or radishes for extra crunch and flavor.
- **Make-Ahead**: The salad and dressing can be made ahead of time and stored separately. Combine just before serving to keep everything fresh.

Enjoy your fresh and flavorful Greek Salad with Chicken!

Spaghetti and Meatballs

Ingredients:

For the Meatballs:

- **Ground beef**: 1 lb (you can also use a mix of beef and pork)
- **Breadcrumbs**: 1 cup (preferably Italian-seasoned or plain)
- **Egg**: 1 large
- **Parmesan cheese**: 1/2 cup, grated
- **Parsley**: 1/4 cup, chopped (fresh)
- **Garlic**: 2 cloves, minced
- **Salt**: 1 tsp
- **Black pepper**: 1/2 tsp
- **Red pepper flakes**: 1/4 tsp (optional, for heat)
- **Milk**: 1/4 cup (to moisten the breadcrumbs)

For the Sauce:

- **Olive oil**: 2 tbsp
- **Onion**: 1 medium, finely chopped
- **Garlic**: 3 cloves, minced
- **Canned tomatoes**: 2 (15 oz each) cans of crushed tomatoes
- **Tomato paste**: 2 tbsp
- **Dried basil**: 1 tsp
- **Dried oregano**: 1 tsp
- **Sugar**: 1 tsp (optional, to balance acidity)
- **Salt and pepper**: To taste

For the Spaghetti:

- **Spaghetti**: 12 oz (or enough for 4 servings)
- **Salt**: For the pasta water

To Serve:

- **Parmesan cheese**: Freshly grated
- **Fresh basil or parsley**: Chopped (optional, for garnish)

Instructions:

1. **Prepare the Meatballs:**
   - Preheat your oven to 375°F (190°C).

- In a large bowl, combine ground beef, breadcrumbs, egg, Parmesan cheese, parsley, minced garlic, salt, pepper, and red pepper flakes.
- Add milk to moisten the breadcrumbs and mix until well combined. Avoid over-mixing to keep the meatballs tender.
- Shape the mixture into 1.5-inch meatballs and place them on a baking sheet lined with parchment paper or a lightly greased rack.

2. **Bake the Meatballs:**
    - Bake in the preheated oven for 20-25 minutes, or until the meatballs are cooked through and have an internal temperature of 160°F (71°C). You can also cook them in a skillet with a bit of oil if you prefer.
3. **Make the Sauce:**
    - While the meatballs are baking, heat olive oil in a large skillet or saucepan over medium heat.
    - Add chopped onion and cook until softened, about 5 minutes.
    - Add minced garlic and cook for another minute.
    - Stir in crushed tomatoes and tomato paste. Add dried basil, oregano, sugar (if using), salt, and pepper.
    - Simmer the sauce over low heat for about 15-20 minutes, stirring occasionally. Adjust seasoning as needed.
4. **Cook the Spaghetti:**
    - Bring a large pot of salted water to a boil.
    - Cook the spaghetti according to package instructions until al dente.
    - Drain the spaghetti and toss with a little olive oil to prevent sticking if not serving immediately.
5. **Combine and Serve:**
    - Add the baked meatballs to the sauce and let them simmer together for an additional 5-10 minutes to absorb flavors.
    - Serve the meatballs and sauce over the cooked spaghetti.
    - Garnish with freshly grated Parmesan cheese and chopped basil or parsley if desired.

Tips:

- **Make-Ahead**: You can prepare the meatballs and sauce ahead of time. Store separately in the refrigerator for up to 3 days or freeze for longer storage.
- **Meatballs Variations**: For extra flavor, you can add finely chopped onions or bell peppers to the meatball mixture.
- **Sauce Variations**: Feel free to add a splash of red wine or a pinch of chili flakes for additional depth and heat.

Enjoy your hearty and delicious Spaghetti and Meatballs!

Fish Tacos

Ingredients:

For the Fish:

- **White fish**: 1 lb (such as cod, tilapia, or mahi-mahi), cut into strips
- **Flour**: 1/2 cup
- **Cornstarch**: 1/4 cup
- **Paprika**: 1 tsp
- **Cumin**: 1/2 tsp
- **Garlic powder**: 1/2 tsp
- **Onion powder**: 1/2 tsp
- **Salt**: 1/2 tsp
- **Black pepper**: 1/4 tsp
- **Egg**: 1 large, beaten
- **Panko breadcrumbs**: 1 cup (for coating)
- **Vegetable oil**: For frying (or you can use an air fryer or bake)

For the Slaw:

- **Shredded cabbage**: 3 cups (green, red, or a mix)
- **Carrots**: 1 cup, shredded
- **Green onions**: 2, sliced
- **Cilantro**: 1/4 cup, chopped

For the Slaw Dressing:

- **Mayonnaise**: 1/2 cup
- **Sour cream**: 1/4 cup
- **Lime juice**: 2 tbsp (freshly squeezed)
- **Honey**: 1 tbsp
- **Salt**: To taste
- **Black pepper**: To taste

For the Tacos:

- **Tortillas**: 8 small (corn or flour)
- **Lime wedges**: For serving
- **Fresh cilantro**: For garnish

Instructions:

1. **Prepare the Fish:**

- In a shallow bowl, mix flour, cornstarch, paprika, cumin, garlic powder, onion powder, salt, and pepper.
- Dip the fish strips into the beaten egg, then coat with the flour mixture.
- Dredge the coated fish in panko breadcrumbs, pressing gently to adhere.
- Heat vegetable oil in a large skillet over medium heat. Fry the fish strips in batches until golden brown and cooked through, about 2-3 minutes per side. Drain on paper towels.

2. **Make the Slaw:**
   - In a large bowl, combine shredded cabbage, shredded carrots, green onions, and chopped cilantro.
   - In a separate small bowl, whisk together mayonnaise, sour cream, lime juice, honey, salt, and pepper.
   - Toss the slaw with the dressing until evenly coated.
3. **Warm the Tortillas:**
   - Heat the tortillas in a dry skillet over medium heat for about 30 seconds on each side, or until warm and pliable. Alternatively, you can wrap them in foil and warm them in the oven.
4. **Assemble the Tacos:**
   - Place a few pieces of the crispy fish onto each tortilla.
   - Top with a generous portion of the slaw.
   - Garnish with additional fresh cilantro if desired.
5. **Serve:**
   - Serve the fish tacos with lime wedges on the side for squeezing over the top.

Tips:

- **Fish Variations**: You can use other types of fish or even shrimp if you prefer.
- **Cooking Method**: For a lighter option, you can bake the fish at 400°F (200°C) for about 12-15 minutes, or use an air fryer for a crispy result with less oil.
- **Slaw Variations**: Add sliced jalapeños or radishes to the slaw for extra flavor and crunch.

Enjoy your fresh and flavorful Fish Tacos!

Pork Tacos with Salsa Verde

Ingredients:

For the Pork:

- **Pork shoulder**: 2 lbs (also known as pork butt), trimmed and cut into chunks
- **Olive oil**: 2 tbsp
- **Garlic**: 4 cloves, minced
- **Cumin**: 1 tsp
- **Chili powder**: 1 tsp
- **Paprika**: 1/2 tsp
- **Oregano**: 1/2 tsp
- **Salt**: 1 tsp
- **Black pepper**: 1/2 tsp
- **Onion**: 1 medium, chopped
- **Chicken broth**: 1 cup (or water)

For the Salsa Verde:

- **Tomatillos**: 1 lb, husked and rinsed
- **Green chilies**: 1-2 (such as jalapeño or serrano), seeded and chopped
- **Garlic**: 2 cloves, peeled
- **Onion**: 1/2, chopped
- **Cilantro**: 1/4 cup, chopped
- **Lime juice**: 2 tbsp (freshly squeezed)
- **Salt**: To taste

For the Tacos:

- **Tortillas**: 8 small (corn or flour)
- **Fresh cilantro**: For garnish
- **Diced onions**: For garnish
- **Lime wedges**: For serving
- **Radishes**: Thinly sliced (optional, for garnish)

Instructions:

1. **Cook the Pork:**
    - In a large skillet or Dutch oven, heat olive oil over medium-high heat.
    - Add the pork chunks and sear on all sides until browned. This should take about 5-7 minutes.
    - Add minced garlic, cumin, chili powder, paprika, oregano, salt, and black pepper. Stir to coat the pork with the spices.

- Add chopped onion and cook for another 2-3 minutes until softened.
- Pour in the chicken broth and bring to a simmer.
- Reduce the heat to low, cover, and cook for about 2-3 hours, or until the pork is very tender and easily shreddable. Alternatively, you can cook the pork in a slow cooker on low for 6-8 hours.
- Once the pork is tender, shred it using two forks. Stir well to mix with the juices.

2. **Make the Salsa Verde:**
   - Preheat your oven's broiler.
   - Place tomatillos, green chilies, and garlic on a baking sheet. Broil for about 5-7 minutes, or until the tomatillos are charred and softened.
   - Transfer the roasted tomatillos, chilies, and garlic to a blender or food processor. Add the chopped onion, cilantro, lime juice, and a pinch of salt.
   - Blend until smooth. Taste and adjust seasoning as needed.

3. **Warm the Tortillas:**
   - Heat the tortillas in a dry skillet over medium heat for about 30 seconds on each side, or until warm and pliable. You can also wrap them in foil and warm them in the oven.

4. **Assemble the Tacos:**
   - Place a generous amount of shredded pork onto each tortilla.
   - Top with a spoonful of salsa verde.
   - Garnish with fresh cilantro, diced onions, and radishes if using.

5. **Serve:**
   - Serve the tacos immediately with lime wedges on the side for squeezing over the top.

Tips:

- **Salsa Verde**: For a smoky flavor, you can roast the tomatillos and chilies until charred, or even grill them if preferred.
- **Pork Variations**: You can use other cuts of pork, like pork loin or ribs, but cooking times will vary.
- **Make-Ahead**: The pork and salsa verde can be made ahead of time. Store them separately in the refrigerator and reheat before serving.

Enjoy your flavorful and zesty Pork Tacos with Salsa Verde!

BBQ Chicken Pizza

Ingredients:

For the Pizza:

- **Pizza dough**: 1 lb (store-bought or homemade; enough for one large pizza or two smaller pizzas)
- **BBQ sauce**: 1/2 cup (your favorite brand or homemade)
- **Cooked chicken**: 1 1/2 cups, shredded or diced (grilled, rotisserie, or leftover chicken works well)
- **Red onion**: 1/2, thinly sliced
- **Mozzarella cheese**: 1 1/2 cups, shredded
- **Cheddar cheese**: 1/2 cup, shredded
- **Fresh cilantro**: 2 tbsp, chopped (for garnish)
- **Olive oil**: 1-2 tbsp (for brushing the crust)

Optional Toppings:

- **Jalapeños**: Thinly sliced (for a spicy kick)
- **Bell peppers**: Thinly sliced (for extra crunch and flavor)

Instructions:

1. **Prepare the Oven and Pizza Dough:**
    - Preheat your oven to 475°F (245°C) or higher if your oven can go hotter. If using a pizza stone, place it in the oven to preheat as well.
    - Roll out the pizza dough on a floured surface to your desired thickness. Transfer the rolled dough to a parchment-lined pizza peel or baking sheet if not using a pizza stone.
2. **Prepare the Chicken:**
    - In a bowl, toss the cooked chicken with 1/4 cup of BBQ sauce until evenly coated. Set aside.
3. **Assemble the Pizza:**
    - Brush the pizza dough with olive oil to prevent it from getting soggy.
    - Spread the remaining 1/4 cup of BBQ sauce evenly over the dough, leaving a small border around the edges.
    - Scatter the BBQ chicken evenly over the sauce.
    - Add thinly sliced red onions and any optional toppings like jalapeños or bell peppers.
    - Sprinkle mozzarella and cheddar cheese evenly over the top.
4. **Bake the Pizza:**

- Transfer the pizza to the preheated oven (or onto the pizza stone if using) and bake for 12-15 minutes, or until the crust is golden brown and the cheese is bubbly and melted.

5. **Garnish and Serve:**
    - Remove the pizza from the oven and let it cool for a few minutes.
    - Sprinkle fresh cilantro over the top for a burst of flavor.
    - Slice and serve immediately.

Tips:

- **BBQ Sauce**: Choose a BBQ sauce that you enjoy the flavor of. You can also make your own if you prefer a customized taste.
- **Chicken**: Shredded rotisserie chicken is a great time-saver and adds extra flavor.
- **Crust**: For a crispier crust, pre-bake the pizza dough for 5 minutes before adding the toppings.
- **Garnishes**: Experiment with other garnishes like sliced green onions or a drizzle of extra BBQ sauce.

Enjoy your homemade BBQ Chicken Pizza!

Veggie Burger

Ingredients:

For the Veggie Patties:

- **Canned black beans**: 1 (15 oz) can, drained and rinsed
- **Carrot**: 1 medium, grated
- **Red bell pepper**: 1/2, finely diced
- **Onion**: 1/2, finely diced
- **Garlic**: 2 cloves, minced
- **Rolled oats**: 1/2 cup
- **Breadcrumbs**: 1/4 cup (or more if needed)
- **Flaxseed meal**: 2 tbsp (for binding; optional)
- **Egg**: 1 (or use a flax egg for a vegan version; mix 1 tbsp flaxseed meal with 3 tbsp water and let sit for 5 minutes)
- **Cumin**: 1 tsp
- **Paprika**: 1/2 tsp
- **Chili powder**: 1/2 tsp
- **Salt**: 1/2 tsp
- **Black pepper**: 1/4 tsp
- **Olive oil**: For cooking

For Serving:

- **Burger buns**: 4
- **Lettuce**: For topping
- **Tomato**: Sliced
- **Red onion**: Sliced
- **Pickles**: Optional
- **Cheese**: Slices (optional; use vegan cheese for a vegan version)
- **Condiments**: Ketchup, mustard, mayonnaise, or your favorite sauce

Instructions:

1. **Prepare the Veggie Mixture:**
   - In a large bowl, mash the black beans with a fork or potato masher until mostly smooth, with some chunks remaining for texture.
   - Add the grated carrot, diced red bell pepper, diced onion, minced garlic, rolled oats, breadcrumbs, flaxseed meal (if using), and the egg.
   - Stir in cumin, paprika, chili powder, salt, and black pepper. Mix until well combined.
2. **Form the Patties:**

- Shape the mixture into 4 patties, about 1/2 inch thick. If the mixture is too wet and not holding together, add more breadcrumbs a tablespoon at a time until the mixture is firmer.
3. **Cook the Patties:**
    - Heat a little olive oil in a skillet over medium heat.
    - Cook the patties for about 5-7 minutes on each side, or until they are golden brown and crispy on the outside. You can also bake them at 375°F (190°C) for 20-25 minutes, flipping halfway through, for a lower-fat option.
4. **Assemble the Burgers:**
    - Toast the burger buns if desired.
    - Place each veggie patty on the bottom half of a bun.
    - Top with lettuce, tomato slices, red onion slices, pickles, cheese (if using), and your preferred condiments.
    - Place the top bun over the toppings.
5. **Serve:**
    - Serve immediately with your favorite side dishes like sweet potato fries, salad, or coleslaw.

Tips:

- **Variations**: Feel free to customize the patties by adding ingredients like corn, mushrooms, or chopped spinach for extra flavor and nutrition.
- **Binding**: If the mixture is too dry, add a bit of water or extra flaxseed meal; if too wet, add more breadcrumbs.
- **Freezing**: These patties freeze well. To freeze, place uncooked patties on a baking sheet and freeze until solid, then transfer to a freezer bag. Cook from frozen or thaw before cooking.

Enjoy your homemade Veggie Burgers!

Clubhouse Chicken Sandwich

Ingredients:

For the Chicken:

- **Chicken breasts**: 2, boneless and skinless
- **Olive oil**: 2 tbsp
- **Paprika**: 1 tsp
- **Garlic powder**: 1/2 tsp
- **Onion powder**: 1/2 tsp
- **Salt**: 1/2 tsp
- **Black pepper**: 1/4 tsp
- **Lemon juice**: 1 tbsp (optional, for marinating)

For the Sandwich:

- **Bacon**: 4 slices
- **Lettuce**: 4-6 leaves (romaine or iceberg work well)
- **Tomato**: 1 large, sliced
- **Avocado**: 1, sliced (optional)
- **Cheddar cheese**: 2 slices (optional)
- **Mayonnaise**: 2-3 tbsp
- **Mustard**: 1-2 tbsp (optional)
- **Bread**: 6 slices (white, whole wheat, or your choice), toasted

Instructions:

1. **Prepare the Chicken:**
    - Preheat your grill or skillet to medium-high heat.
    - Season the chicken breasts with paprika, garlic powder, onion powder, salt, and black pepper. Optionally, you can marinate the chicken in olive oil and lemon juice for 30 minutes to an hour for added flavor.
    - Brush the grill or skillet with a little olive oil.
    - Grill or cook the chicken for 6-7 minutes per side, or until the internal temperature reaches 165°F (74°C). Let the chicken rest for a few minutes before slicing it into strips.
2. **Cook the Bacon:**
    - While the chicken is cooking, heat a skillet over medium heat.
    - Cook the bacon slices until crispy, about 4-5 minutes per side. Drain on paper towels.
3. **Toast the Bread:**
    - Toast the bread slices in a toaster or on a skillet until golden brown.
4. **Assemble the Sandwiches:**

- Spread mayonnaise (and mustard, if using) on one side of each slice of toasted bread.
- On one slice of bread, layer lettuce, tomato slices, and avocado slices (if using).
- Place a slice of cheddar cheese on top of the vegetables (if using).
- Add a layer of sliced chicken breast and crispy bacon.
- Top with another slice of toasted bread.

5. **Finish and Serve:**
    - Cut the sandwiches in half diagonally and secure with toothpicks if needed.
    - Serve immediately with your favorite side dishes, such as fries, chips, or a salad.

Tips:

- **Chicken Variation**: For a healthier option, you can bake the chicken at 375°F (190°C) for 25-30 minutes or until cooked through.
- **Extra Flavor**: Add pickles or red onions for an extra punch of flavor.
- **Vegetarian Option**: Substitute the chicken with a veggie burger or grilled portobello mushrooms.

Enjoy your delicious Clubhouse Chicken Sandwich!

Lobster Roll

Ingredients:

For the Lobster Filling:

- **Live lobsters**: 2 (about 1.5 lbs each) or pre-cooked lobster meat (about 1 pound)
- **Mayonnaise**: 1/4 cup
- **Lemon juice**: 1 tbsp (freshly squeezed)
- **Celery**: 1/2 cup, finely diced
- **Chives**: 2 tbsp, finely chopped
- **Dill**: 1 tbsp, chopped (optional)
- **Salt**: To taste
- **Black pepper**: To taste

For the Rolls:

- **Hot dog rolls**: 4 (New England-style split-top rolls are ideal)
- **Butter**: 2-3 tbsp, melted (for toasting the rolls)
- **Lettuce leaves**: 4 (optional, for lining the rolls)

Instructions:

1. **Cook the Lobster (if using live lobsters):**
   - Bring a large pot of salted water to a boil.
   - Add the live lobsters to the boiling water and cook for about 8-10 minutes, or until the shells are bright red and the lobster meat is opaque.
   - Transfer the lobsters to an ice bath to cool. Once cooled, remove the lobster meat from the shells. Discard the shells and cut the lobster meat into bite-sized pieces.
2. **Prepare the Lobster Filling:**
   - In a bowl, combine the lobster meat, mayonnaise, lemon juice, diced celery, chives, and dill (if using).
   - Season with salt and pepper to taste. Mix gently until all ingredients are well combined. Avoid over-mixing to keep the lobster chunks intact.
3. **Toast the Rolls:**
   - Preheat a skillet over medium heat.
   - Brush the inside of each hot dog roll with melted butter.
   - Place the rolls, buttered side down, in the skillet and cook until golden brown and crispy. Alternatively, you can toast them under a broiler, but watch closely to avoid burning.
4. **Assemble the Lobster Rolls:**
   - If desired, place a leaf of lettuce inside each toasted roll to line it.
   - Spoon the lobster filling into each roll, heaping it generously.

5. **Serve:**
   - Serve the Lobster Rolls immediately, with additional lemon wedges on the side if desired.

Tips:

- **Lobster Meat**: For a quicker version, you can use pre-cooked lobster meat. Just be sure to check that it's fresh or properly thawed if frozen.
- **Seasoning**: Adjust the amount of mayonnaise and lemon juice to your taste. Some people prefer a creamier filling, while others like it lighter.
- **Butter**: For an extra touch, you can add a sprinkle of Old Bay seasoning to the butter before toasting the rolls.

Enjoy your classic Lobster Roll, a delicious and indulgent treat!

Chicken Parmesan Sandwich

Ingredients:

For the Chicken:

- **Chicken breasts**: 2, boneless and skinless
- **Flour**: 1/2 cup
- **Egg**: 1 large
- **Breadcrumbs**: 1 cup (preferably Italian-seasoned or plain mixed with dried herbs)
- **Parmesan cheese**: 1/4 cup, grated (for mixing with breadcrumbs)
- **Salt**: 1/2 tsp
- **Black pepper**: 1/4 tsp
- **Olive oil**: For frying

For the Sauce:

- **Olive oil**: 1 tbsp
- **Garlic**: 2 cloves, minced
- **Canned crushed tomatoes**: 1 (15 oz) can
- **Tomato paste**: 2 tbsp
- **Dried basil**: 1 tsp
- **Dried oregano**: 1/2 tsp
- **Sugar**: 1 tsp (optional, to balance acidity)
- **Salt and pepper**: To taste

For the Sandwich:

- **Sub rolls or Italian hoagie rolls**: 4
- **Mozzarella cheese**: 4 slices (or shredded)
- **Fresh basil**: For garnish (optional)
- **Parmesan cheese**: Extra for sprinkling (optional)

Instructions:

1. **Prepare the Chicken:**
    - Preheat your oven to 375°F (190°C).
    - Place the chicken breasts between two sheets of plastic wrap or parchment paper. Pound them to an even thickness using a meat mallet or rolling pin.
    - Set up a breading station:
        - Place flour in one shallow dish.
        - Beat the egg in another shallow dish.
        - Combine breadcrumbs, grated Parmesan, salt, and pepper in a third shallow dish.

- Dredge each chicken breast in flour, shaking off excess. Dip in the beaten egg, then coat with the breadcrumb mixture, pressing gently to adhere.

2. **Cook the Chicken:**
    - Heat a few tablespoons of olive oil in a skillet over medium heat.
    - Fry the chicken breasts for 4-5 minutes per side, or until golden brown and cooked through (internal temperature should be 165°F or 74°C). They will finish cooking in the oven, so they don't need to be fully cooked at this stage.
    - Transfer the chicken to a baking sheet.
3. **Prepare the Sauce:**
    - In a saucepan, heat olive oil over medium heat.
    - Add minced garlic and sauté for about 1 minute, or until fragrant.
    - Stir in crushed tomatoes and tomato paste. Add dried basil, oregano, and sugar if using.
    - Simmer the sauce for 10-15 minutes, stirring occasionally. Season with salt and pepper to taste.
4. **Assemble the Sandwiches:**
    - Spoon a bit of sauce over each chicken breast on the baking sheet.
    - Place a slice of mozzarella cheese on top of each chicken breast.
    - Bake in the preheated oven for 5-10 minutes, or until the cheese is melted and bubbly.
5. **Prepare the Rolls:**
    - If desired, toast the sub rolls lightly in the oven or a toaster.
6. **Assemble the Sandwiches:**
    - Spread a thin layer of sauce on the inside of each roll.
    - Place a cheesy chicken breast in each roll.
    - Top with a sprinkle of extra Parmesan cheese and fresh basil if desired.
7. **Serve:**
    - Serve the Chicken Parmesan Sandwiches warm, with extra sauce on the side if desired.

Tips:

- **Chicken Breading**: For extra crispiness, you can double-coat the chicken (dredge, egg, breadcrumb, egg, breadcrumb).
- **Sauce**: Make the sauce ahead of time and refrigerate it; it can be kept for up to a week.
- **Cheese**: For a richer flavor, you can use provolone cheese along with or instead of mozzarella.

Enjoy your delicious Chicken Parmesan Sandwich!

Chili Con Carne

Ingredients:

For the Chili:

- **Ground beef**: 1 lb (or use ground turkey or a mix of meats if preferred)
- **Onion**: 1 large, diced
- **Garlic**: 3 cloves, minced
- **Bell peppers**: 1-2, diced (red, green, or a mix)
- **Tomato paste**: 2 tbsp
- **Canned diced tomatoes**: 1 (14.5 oz) can
- **Canned kidney beans**: 1 (15 oz) can, drained and rinsed (or black beans, pinto beans, or a mix)
- **Beef broth**: 1 cup (or chicken or vegetable broth)
- **Chili powder**: 2 tbsp
- **Cumin**: 1 tsp
- **Paprika**: 1 tsp
- **Oregano**: 1/2 tsp
- **Cayenne pepper**: 1/4 tsp (optional, for extra heat)
- **Salt**: To taste
- **Black pepper**: To taste
- **Olive oil**: 2 tbsp (for sautéing)

For Garnishing (optional):

- **Shredded cheese**: Cheddar, Monterey Jack, or your choice
- **Chopped fresh cilantro**: For freshness
- **Sour cream**: For creaminess
- **Sliced jalapeños**: For extra heat
- **Sliced green onions**: For garnish
- **Chopped avocado**: For added richness

Instructions:

1. **Cook the Beef:**
    - In a large pot or Dutch oven, heat olive oil over medium heat.
    - Add diced onion and cook until translucent, about 5 minutes.
    - Add minced garlic and cook for another 1 minute.
    - Add ground beef and cook, breaking it up with a spoon, until browned and fully cooked. Drain excess fat if needed.
2. **Add Vegetables and Spices:**
    - Stir in diced bell peppers and cook for about 3-4 minutes until they start to soften.
    - Add tomato paste and cook for 2 minutes to deepen its flavor.

- Add chili powder, cumin, paprika, oregano, and cayenne pepper (if using). Stir to coat the meat and vegetables with the spices.
3. **Add Liquids and Beans:**
    - Stir in canned diced tomatoes, beef broth, and drained beans.
    - Bring the mixture to a simmer.
4. **Simmer the Chili:**
    - Reduce the heat to low and let the chili simmer uncovered for 20-30 minutes, stirring occasionally. This allows the flavors to meld together and the chili to thicken.
    - Taste and adjust seasoning with salt and pepper as needed. If the chili is too thick, add a bit more broth or water.
5. **Serve:**
    - Ladle the chili into bowls and garnish with your choice of toppings like shredded cheese, chopped cilantro, sour cream, sliced jalapeños, green onions, or avocado.
    - Serve with cornbread, rice, or tortilla chips on the side.

Tips:

- **Flavor Development**: For even more depth of flavor, you can let the chili simmer for up to an hour, or make it a day ahead and refrigerate. Chili often tastes better the next day.
- **Meat Variations**: You can use other meats like ground turkey, chicken, or even a combination of meats. For a vegetarian version, simply omit the meat and use additional beans or lentils.
- **Spice Levels**: Adjust the heat by varying the amount of cayenne pepper or adding chopped fresh chili peppers.

Enjoy your flavorful and hearty Chili Con Carne!

Beef Stroganoff

Ingredients:

For the Beef:

- **Beef sirloin or tenderloin**: 1 lb, thinly sliced into strips (or use beef stew meat, cut into smaller pieces)
- **Salt**: 1/2 tsp
- **Black pepper**: 1/2 tsp
- **Flour**: 2 tbsp (for coating the beef)

For the Sauce:

- **Butter**: 2 tbsp
- **Olive oil**: 2 tbsp
- **Onion**: 1 medium, finely diced
- **Garlic**: 2 cloves, minced
- **Mushrooms**: 8 oz, sliced (button or cremini mushrooms work well)
- **Beef broth**: 1 cup
- **White wine**: 1/2 cup (optional; can use additional beef broth if preferred)
- **Dijon mustard**: 1 tbsp
- **Worcestershire sauce**: 1 tbsp
- **Sour cream**: 1 cup
- **Parsley**: 2 tbsp, chopped (for garnish)
- **Cornstarch**: 1-2 tsp (optional, for thickening)

For Serving:

- **Egg noodles**: 12 oz (or rice, for serving)
- **Salt and pepper**: To taste

Instructions:

1. **Prepare the Beef:**
    - Season the beef strips with salt and pepper. Coat lightly with flour, shaking off excess.
    - Heat 1 tablespoon of olive oil and 1 tablespoon of butter in a large skillet or Dutch oven over medium-high heat.
    - Add the beef in batches (do not overcrowd the pan) and cook until browned on all sides. Transfer the beef to a plate and set aside.
2. **Make the Sauce:**
    - In the same skillet, add the remaining 1 tablespoon of olive oil and 1 tablespoon of butter.

- Add diced onion and cook until softened, about 4-5 minutes.
- Add minced garlic and cook for another 1 minute.
- Add the sliced mushrooms and cook until they release their juices and become browned, about 5-7 minutes.

3. **Deglaze and Simmer:**
   - Pour in the white wine (if using) and scrape up any browned bits from the bottom of the pan. Let it simmer for 2-3 minutes to reduce slightly.
   - Stir in the beef broth, Dijon mustard, and Worcestershire sauce. Bring the mixture to a simmer.

4. **Combine and Finish:**
   - Return the browned beef to the skillet, along with any juices that have accumulated on the plate.
   - Reduce heat to low and let the mixture simmer for about 10 minutes, or until the beef is tender and the sauce has thickened slightly. If using cornstarch, mix 1-2 teaspoons with a little water and stir into the sauce to thicken.
   - Stir in the sour cream and heat through, but do not let it boil to prevent curdling. Adjust seasoning with salt and pepper to taste.

5. **Prepare the Noodles or Rice:**
   - While the sauce is simmering, cook the egg noodles or rice according to package instructions. Drain well.

6. **Serve:**
   - Serve the Beef Stroganoff over the cooked egg noodles or rice.
   - Garnish with chopped parsley.

Tips:

- **Beef Choice**: For the most tender beef, use a cut like sirloin or tenderloin. Avoid overcooking to keep the beef tender.
- **Cream**: If you prefer a richer sauce, you can use heavy cream instead of sour cream, though it will alter the traditional flavor slightly.
- **Mushrooms**: For a deeper mushroom flavor, you can use a mix of fresh mushrooms and dried porcini mushrooms.

Enjoy your classic Beef Stroganoff—a comforting and creamy dish that's sure to please!

Chicken Tortilla Soup

Ingredients:

For the Soup:

- **Chicken breasts or thighs**: 1 lb, boneless and skinless (or use pre-cooked shredded chicken)
- **Olive oil**: 2 tbsp
- **Onion**: 1 medium, diced
- **Garlic**: 3 cloves, minced
- **Bell peppers**: 1-2, diced (any color)
- **Carrot**: 1 large, diced
- **Celery**: 2 stalks, diced
- **Canned diced tomatoes**: 1 (14.5 oz) can
- **Chicken broth**: 4 cups
- **Canned black beans**: 1 (15 oz) can, drained and rinsed
- **Corn**: 1 cup (fresh, frozen, or canned)
- **Taco seasoning**: 2 tbsp (or use a mix of chili powder, cumin, and paprika)
- **Ground cumin**: 1 tsp
- **Paprika**: 1/2 tsp
- **Dried oregano**: 1/2 tsp
- **Salt**: To taste
- **Black pepper**: To taste
- **Lime juice**: 2 tbsp (freshly squeezed)

For Garnishing:

- **Tortilla strips**: Homemade or store-bought
- **Shredded cheese**: Cheddar or Monterey Jack
- **Fresh cilantro**: Chopped
- **Avocado**: Diced
- **Sour cream**: Optional
- **Sliced jalapeños**: Optional

Instructions:

1. **Cook the Chicken:**
    - If using raw chicken, cook the chicken breasts or thighs in a large pot with a little oil or water until fully cooked. You can also use pre-cooked or shredded chicken for convenience.
    - Once cooked, shred the chicken using two forks and set aside.
2. **Prepare the Soup Base:**
    - In a large pot or Dutch oven, heat olive oil over medium heat.

- Add the diced onion, bell peppers, carrot, and celery. Cook until the vegetables are softened, about 5-7 minutes.
- Add minced garlic and cook for another 1 minute, until fragrant.

3. **Build the Soup:**
    - Stir in the taco seasoning, ground cumin, paprika, and dried oregano. Cook for 1-2 minutes to toast the spices.
    - Add the canned diced tomatoes and chicken broth. Bring the mixture to a boil.
    - Reduce the heat and simmer for 10 minutes.

4. **Add Chicken and Beans:**
    - Stir in the shredded chicken, black beans, and corn. Continue to simmer for another 5 minutes, or until the soup is heated through and flavors are well combined.
    - Add lime juice and season with salt and pepper to taste.

5. **Serve:**
    - Ladle the soup into bowls.
    - Top with tortilla strips, shredded cheese, chopped cilantro, diced avocado, and a dollop of sour cream if desired.
    - Add sliced jalapeños for extra heat if you like.

Tips:

- **Tortilla Strips**: To make homemade tortilla strips, cut corn tortillas into strips, toss with a little oil and salt, and bake at 375°F (190°C) for 10-15 minutes, or until crispy.
- **Chicken**: Using rotisserie chicken or leftover cooked chicken is a great time-saver and adds extra flavor.
- **Spices**: Adjust the seasoning and spices to your taste. If you prefer a spicier soup, add more chili powder or fresh jalapeños.

Enjoy your hearty and flavorful Chicken Tortilla Soup!

Southwest Beef Chili

Ingredients:

For the Chili:

- **Ground beef**: 1 lb
- **Olive oil**: 2 tbsp
- **Onion**: 1 large, diced
- **Garlic**: 3 cloves, minced
- **Bell peppers**: 1-2, diced (any color)
- **Carrot**: 1 large, diced
- **Celery**: 2 stalks, diced
- **Canned diced tomatoes**: 1 (14.5 oz) can
- **Canned tomato sauce**: 1 (8 oz) can
- **Canned kidney beans**: 1 (15 oz) can, drained and rinsed
- **Canned black beans**: 1 (15 oz) can, drained and rinsed
- **Corn**: 1 cup (fresh, frozen, or canned)
- **Beef broth**: 1 cup
- **Chili powder**: 2 tbsp
- **Ground cumin**: 1 tbsp
- **Paprika**: 1 tsp
- **Dried oregano**: 1/2 tsp
- **Cayenne pepper**: 1/4 tsp (optional, for extra heat)
- **Salt**: To taste
- **Black pepper**: To taste
- **Lime juice**: 1-2 tbsp (for a touch of brightness)

For Garnishing (optional):

- **Shredded cheese**: Cheddar or Monterey Jack
- **Chopped fresh cilantro**: For garnish
- **Sour cream**: For creaminess
- **Sliced jalapeños**: For extra heat
- **Chopped avocado**: For added richness
- **Tortilla chips**: For crunch

Instructions:

1. **Cook the Beef:**
   - In a large pot or Dutch oven, heat olive oil over medium heat.
   - Add the ground beef and cook, breaking it up with a spoon, until browned and fully cooked. Drain excess fat if needed.
2. **Add Vegetables and Spices:**

- Add diced onion, bell peppers, carrot, and celery to the pot. Cook until the vegetables are softened, about 5-7 minutes.
- Add minced garlic and cook for another 1 minute, until fragrant.
3. **Build the Chili:**
    - Stir in chili powder, ground cumin, paprika, dried oregano, and cayenne pepper (if using). Cook for 1-2 minutes to toast the spices.
    - Add canned diced tomatoes, tomato sauce, and beef broth. Stir to combine.
    - Bring the mixture to a boil, then reduce the heat and simmer for 10 minutes.
4. **Add Beans and Corn:**
    - Stir in the kidney beans, black beans, and corn. Simmer for an additional 10-15 minutes, or until the chili is thickened and the flavors are well combined.
    - Add lime juice and season with salt and pepper to taste.
5. **Serve:**
    - Ladle the chili into bowls.
    - Garnish with shredded cheese, chopped cilantro, sour cream, sliced jalapeños, and chopped avocado if desired.
    - Serve with tortilla chips or over rice for a complete meal.

Tips:

- **Beef Variations**: You can use ground turkey or chicken for a lighter version, or a mix of different ground meats.
- **Spice Level**: Adjust the amount of cayenne pepper and chili powder to suit your heat preference.
- **Flavor Enhancement**: For a richer flavor, you can let the chili simmer for longer or make it a day ahead. It often tastes even better the next day.

Enjoy your hearty and flavorful Southwest Beef Chili!

Tuna Salad Sandwich

Ingredients:

- **1 can of tuna** (5 oz), drained
- **2 tablespoons mayonnaise**
- **1 tablespoon Dijon mustard** (optional)
- **1 celery stalk**, finely chopped
- **1/4 small red onion**, finely chopped
- **Salt and pepper**, to taste
- **2 slices of bread** (whole wheat, sourdough, or your choice)
- **Lettuce leaves** (optional)
- **Tomato slices** (optional)

Instructions:

1. **Prepare the Tuna Salad:**
    - In a medium bowl, combine the drained tuna, mayonnaise, and Dijon mustard (if using). Mix well.
    - Add the chopped celery and red onion. Stir to combine.
    - Season with salt and pepper to taste.
2. **Assemble the Sandwich:**
    - Lay out the bread slices. If you like, you can toast them lightly.
    - Spread the tuna salad evenly over one slice of bread.
    - Top with lettuce leaves and tomato slices if you're using them.
    - Place the other slice of bread on top.
3. **Serve:**
    - Cut the sandwich in half if desired and serve immediately.

Feel free to adjust the ingredients to suit your taste. Some people like to add a bit of lemon juice, pickles, or hard-boiled eggs for extra flavor and texture. Enjoy your sandwich!

Asian Chicken Salad

Ingredients:

For the Salad:

- **2 cups cooked chicken** (shredded or diced; rotisserie chicken works great)
- **4 cups mixed greens** (such as romaine, spinach, or cabbage)
- **1 cup shredded carrots**
- **1 cup sliced bell peppers** (red or yellow)
- **1/2 cup edamame** (cooked and shelled)
- **1/2 cup cucumber**, thinly sliced
- **1/4 cup green onions**, sliced
- **1/4 cup chopped cilantro** (optional)
- **1/4 cup sliced almonds** (optional)
- **1/4 cup sesame seeds** (optional)

For the Dressing:

- **1/4 cup soy sauce**
- **2 tablespoons rice vinegar**
- **2 tablespoons sesame oil**
- **1 tablespoon honey** (or maple syrup for a vegan option)
- **1 tablespoon grated fresh ginger**
- **1 clove garlic**, minced
- **1 teaspoon Sriracha** (optional, for a bit of heat)

Instructions:

1. **Prepare the Dressing:**
   - In a small bowl, whisk together the soy sauce, rice vinegar, sesame oil, honey, grated ginger, minced garlic, and Sriracha (if using). Adjust seasoning to taste, and set aside.
2. **Prepare the Salad:**
   - In a large bowl, combine the mixed greens, shredded carrots, sliced bell peppers, edamame, cucumber, and green onions.
   - Add the shredded chicken on top.
3. **Add the Dressing:**
   - Drizzle the dressing over the salad and toss gently to combine. Make sure all ingredients are well-coated with the dressing.
4. **Garnish and Serve:**
   - If desired, sprinkle with chopped cilantro, sliced almonds, and sesame seeds.
   - Serve immediately or chill in the refrigerator for a bit before serving.

This salad is quite versatile, so feel free to add or substitute ingredients based on your preferences or what you have on hand. Enjoy your Asian Chicken Salad!

Crispy Chicken Tenders

Ingredients:

For the Chicken:

- **1 lb chicken tenders** (or chicken breasts cut into strips)
- **1 cup all-purpose flour**
- **1 teaspoon paprika**
- **1 teaspoon garlic powder**
- **1/2 teaspoon onion powder**
- **1/2 teaspoon salt**
- **1/4 teaspoon black pepper**
- **2 large eggs**
- **1 cup breadcrumbs** (panko or regular)
- **1/2 cup grated Parmesan cheese** (optional)
- **Vegetable oil** (for frying)

For Dipping Sauce (optional):

- **1/2 cup honey mustard** (mix honey and Dijon mustard to taste)
- **1/2 cup barbecue sauce**
- **1/2 cup ranch dressing**

Instructions:

1. **Prepare the Breading Station:**
   - Set up three shallow dishes: one with flour mixed with paprika, garlic powder, onion powder, salt, and pepper; one with beaten eggs; and one with a mixture of breadcrumbs and Parmesan cheese (if using).
2. **Coat the Chicken:**
   - Dredge each chicken tender in the seasoned flour, shaking off any excess.
   - Dip the floured chicken in the beaten eggs, allowing excess to drip off.
   - Coat the chicken with the breadcrumb mixture, pressing gently to adhere.
3. **Heat the Oil:**
   - In a large skillet, heat about 1/2 inch of vegetable oil over medium heat. The oil is ready when a breadcrumb dropped in sizzles immediately.
4. **Fry the Chicken:**
   - Add the chicken tenders to the skillet in batches, being careful not to overcrowd. Fry for about 3-4 minutes per side, or until golden brown and cooked through (internal temperature should reach 165°F/74°C).
5. **Drain and Serve:**

- Remove the chicken tenders from the skillet and drain on a paper towel-lined plate.
6. **Optional: Make the Dipping Sauces:**
    - Mix honey and Dijon mustard for a sweet and tangy honey mustard sauce.
    - Use store-bought or homemade barbecue sauce.
    - Ranch dressing is always a classic choice.

Serve your crispy chicken tenders hot with your favorite dipping sauces and sides. Enjoy!

Beef Burritos

Ingredients:

For the Beef Filling:

- **1 lb ground beef**
- **1 small onion**, finely chopped
- **2 cloves garlic**, minced
- **1 tablespoon chili powder**
- **1 teaspoon cumin**
- **1/2 teaspoon paprika**
- **1/2 teaspoon onion powder**
- **1/2 teaspoon garlic powder**
- **1/4 teaspoon cayenne pepper** (optional, for heat)
- **1/2 cup beef broth** or water
- **1 can (15 oz) black beans**, drained and rinsed
- **1 cup corn kernels** (fresh, frozen, or canned)
- **Salt and pepper**, to taste

For Assembling the Burritos:

- **4 large flour tortillas** (10-inch size)
- **1 cup shredded cheddar cheese** (or your favorite cheese)
- **1 cup cooked rice** (optional)
- **1/2 cup salsa** (optional, for adding to the filling)
- **1/4 cup chopped fresh cilantro** (optional)
- **Sour cream** (for serving)
- **Guacamole** (for serving)
- **Salsa or hot sauce** (for serving)

Instructions:

1. **Cook the Beef Filling:**
    - In a large skillet, heat a bit of oil over medium heat. Add the chopped onion and cook until softened, about 3-4 minutes.
    - Add the minced garlic and cook for another 30 seconds.
    - Add the ground beef, breaking it up with a spoon, and cook until browned and cooked through. Drain excess fat if necessary.
    - Stir in the chili powder, cumin, paprika, onion powder, garlic powder, and cayenne pepper (if using). Cook for 1-2 minutes to toast the spices.
    - Pour in the beef broth or water and stir, scraping up any browned bits from the bottom of the pan.

- Add the black beans and corn. Cook for another 2-3 minutes, until everything is well combined and heated through. Season with salt and pepper to taste.
2. **Assemble the Burritos:**
    - Warm the flour tortillas in a dry skillet or microwave to make them more pliable.
    - Lay a tortilla flat and spoon some of the beef mixture down the center.
    - Top with shredded cheese, cooked rice (if using), salsa, and chopped cilantro.
    - Fold the sides of the tortilla in, then roll it up from the bottom to enclose the filling.
3. **Optional: Crisp Up the Burritos:**
    - For a crispy finish, heat a bit of oil in a skillet over medium heat. Place the burritos seam-side down and cook until golden and crispy, about 2-3 minutes per side.
4. **Serve:**
    - Serve the beef burritos with sour cream, guacamole, and extra salsa or hot sauce on the side.

These beef burritos are customizable, so feel free to add or swap out ingredients based on your preferences. Enjoy your meal!

Philly Cheesesteak Pizza

Ingredients:

For the Pizza Dough:

- **1 package (2 1/4 teaspoons) active dry yeast**
- **1 cup warm water** (110°F/45°C)
- **2 1/2 cups all-purpose flour**
- **2 tablespoons olive oil**
- **1 teaspoon sugar**
- **1/2 teaspoon salt**

For the Toppings:

- **1 lb ribeye steak** or sirloin, thinly sliced
- **1 tablespoon olive oil**
- **1 small onion**, thinly sliced
- **1 small green bell pepper**, thinly sliced
- **1 small red bell pepper**, thinly sliced
- **1 cup sliced mushrooms** (optional)
- **Salt and pepper**, to taste
- **2 cups shredded provolone cheese** (or a mix of provolone and mozzarella)
- **1/2 cup mayonnaise** (for a creamy sauce, optional)

Instructions:

1. **Prepare the Pizza Dough:**
    - In a small bowl, dissolve the yeast and sugar in warm water. Let sit for about 5 minutes, or until foamy.
    - In a large bowl, combine the flour and salt. Create a well in the center and pour in the yeast mixture and olive oil. Mix until a dough forms.
    - Knead the dough on a floured surface for about 5-7 minutes, until smooth and elastic.
    - Place the dough in a lightly oiled bowl, cover with a damp cloth, and let rise in a warm place for about 1 hour, or until doubled in size.
2. **Prepare the Cheesesteak Toppings:**
    - While the dough is rising, heat olive oil in a skillet over medium-high heat. Add the thinly sliced steak and cook until browned and cooked through, about 3-4 minutes. Remove from the skillet and set aside.
    - In the same skillet, add the onions, bell peppers, and mushrooms (if using). Sauté until softened, about 5-7 minutes. Season with salt and pepper to taste.
3. **Assemble the Pizza:**
    - Preheat your oven to 475°F (245°C) and place a pizza stone or an inverted baking sheet inside to heat.

- Punch down the risen dough and transfer it to a floured surface. Roll out the dough to your desired thickness and shape, then transfer it to a parchment paper-lined pizza peel or another baking sheet.
- If using, spread a thin layer of mayonnaise over the pizza dough as a creamy base sauce.
- Sprinkle a layer of shredded provolone cheese evenly over the dough.
- Distribute the cooked steak evenly over the cheese, followed by the sautéed onions, bell peppers, and mushrooms.
- Top with a bit more cheese if desired.

4. **Bake the Pizza:**
    - Carefully transfer the pizza to the preheated pizza stone or baking sheet in the oven.
    - Bake for 12-15 minutes, or until the crust is golden brown and the cheese is bubbly and melted.

5. **Serve:**
    - Remove the pizza from the oven and let it cool for a few minutes. Slice and serve hot.

Enjoy your Philly Cheesesteak Pizza! It's a great way to enjoy the flavors of a Philly cheesesteak in a fun, pizza form.

Blackened Fish Sandwich

Ingredients:

For the Blackened Fish:

- **4 fish fillets** (such as tilapia, catfish, or cod; about 6 oz each)
- **2 tablespoons paprika**
- **1 teaspoon cayenne pepper** (adjust to taste for heat)
- **1 teaspoon onion powder**
- **1 teaspoon garlic powder**
- **1 teaspoon dried thyme**
- **1 teaspoon dried oregano**
- **1/2 teaspoon salt**
- **1/4 teaspoon black pepper**
- **2 tablespoons olive oil** (for cooking)

For the Sandwich:

- **4 sandwich buns** (such as brioche or ciabatta)
- **1/2 cup mayonnaise**
- **1 tablespoon lemon juice**
- **1 tablespoon Dijon mustard**
- **1 cup shredded lettuce**
- **1 tomato**, sliced
- **Pickles** (optional, for garnish)
- **Lemon wedges** (for serving)

Instructions:

1. **Prepare the Blackened Seasoning:**
   - In a small bowl, mix together the paprika, cayenne pepper, onion powder, garlic powder, thyme, oregano, salt, and black pepper.
2. **Season the Fish:**
   - Pat the fish fillets dry with paper towels. Rub both sides of each fillet with the blackened seasoning mixture, pressing gently to adhere.
3. **Cook the Fish:**
   - Heat olive oil in a large skillet over medium-high heat. Once the oil is hot, add the fish fillets.
   - Cook the fish for about 3-4 minutes per side, or until the fish is cooked through and has a nice blackened crust. The internal temperature should reach 145°F (63°C).
4. **Prepare the Sandwich Condiments:**

- In a small bowl, mix together the mayonnaise, lemon juice, and Dijon mustard.
5. **Assemble the Sandwich:**
    - Toast the sandwich buns lightly if desired.
    - Spread the mayonnaise mixture on the bottom half of each bun.
    - Place a cooked fish fillet on top of the mayo-covered bun.
    - Top with shredded lettuce, tomato slices, and pickles if using.
    - Place the top bun on the sandwich.
6. **Serve:**
    - Serve the Blackened Fish Sandwiches hot, with lemon wedges on the side for a fresh squeeze of lemon juice.

Enjoy your Blackened Fish Sandwich! It's a great balance of spicy, smoky, and fresh flavors.

Classic Macaroni and Cheese

Ingredients:

For the Macaroni:

- **2 cups elbow macaroni** (uncooked)

For the Cheese Sauce:

- **2 tablespoons butter**
- **2 tablespoons all-purpose flour**
- **2 cups milk** (whole milk is best for creaminess)
- **1 cup shredded cheddar cheese** (sharp or mild, as per preference)
- **1 cup shredded mozzarella cheese** (optional, for extra creaminess)
- **1/2 teaspoon salt**
- **1/4 teaspoon black pepper**
- **1/4 teaspoon paprika** (optional, for a bit of smokiness)
- **1/4 teaspoon garlic powder** (optional)

For the Topping (optional):

- **1/2 cup breadcrumbs**
- **2 tablespoons melted butter**
- **1/4 cup grated Parmesan cheese**

Instructions:

1. **Cook the Macaroni:**
    - Bring a large pot of salted water to a boil. Add the elbow macaroni and cook according to the package instructions until al dente. Drain and set aside.
2. **Make the Cheese Sauce:**
    - In a large saucepan or skillet, melt the butter over medium heat.
    - Once the butter is melted, whisk in the flour and cook for about 1-2 minutes, until the mixture is bubbly and slightly golden. This creates a roux that will thicken the sauce.
    - Gradually whisk in the milk, ensuring there are no lumps. Continue to cook, stirring frequently, until the mixture begins to thicken and comes to a gentle simmer, about 5-7 minutes.
    - Reduce the heat to low and add the shredded cheddar cheese (and mozzarella, if using). Stir until the cheese is fully melted and the sauce is smooth.
    - Season the cheese sauce with salt, pepper, paprika, and garlic powder (if using).
3. **Combine Pasta and Sauce:**

- Add the drained macaroni to the cheese sauce. Stir to coat the pasta evenly with the sauce.
4. **Prepare the Topping (optional):**
    - If you like a crispy topping, mix the breadcrumbs with melted butter and grated Parmesan cheese in a small bowl.
5. **Bake (optional):**
    - Preheat your oven to 375°F (190°C).
    - Transfer the macaroni and cheese to a baking dish and spread it out evenly. Sprinkle the breadcrumb mixture evenly over the top.
    - Bake for 20-25 minutes, or until the top is golden brown and the cheese is bubbling.
6. **Serve:**
    - Let the macaroni and cheese cool for a few minutes before serving.

Enjoy your classic macaroni and cheese! It's a timeless comfort food that pairs wonderfully with a simple green salad or steamed vegetables.

Chicken and Waffles

Ingredients:

For the Fried Chicken:

- **4 boneless, skinless chicken breasts** (or thighs if you prefer)
- **1 cup buttermilk**
- **1 cup all-purpose flour**
- **1 teaspoon paprika**
- **1 teaspoon garlic powder**
- **1 teaspoon onion powder**
- **1/2 teaspoon salt**
- **1/2 teaspoon black pepper**
- **1/2 teaspoon cayenne pepper** (optional, for heat)
- **Vegetable oil** (for frying)

For the Waffles:

- **2 cups all-purpose flour**
- **2 tablespoons sugar**
- **1 tablespoon baking powder**
- **1/2 teaspoon salt**
- **2 large eggs**
- **1 3/4 cups milk**
- **1/2 cup melted butter** or vegetable oil
- **1 teaspoon vanilla extract**

For Serving:

- **Maple syrup**
- **Butter**
- **Powdered sugar** (optional, for dusting)
- **Hot sauce** (optional, for the chicken)

Instructions:

1. **Marinate the Chicken:**
   - Place the chicken breasts (or thighs) in a bowl and pour the buttermilk over them. Cover and refrigerate for at least 1 hour, or overnight if possible. This helps tenderize the chicken and adds flavor.
2. **Prepare the Fried Chicken:**

- In a large bowl, mix the flour, paprika, garlic powder, onion powder, salt, black pepper, and cayenne pepper (if using).
- Remove the chicken from the buttermilk, allowing excess to drip off. Dredge each piece in the seasoned flour mixture, coating evenly.
- Heat about 1-2 inches of vegetable oil in a large skillet over medium-high heat to 350°F (175°C).
- Fry the chicken in batches, avoiding overcrowding, for about 6-8 minutes per side, or until golden brown and the internal temperature reaches 165°F (74°C). Drain on paper towels.

3. **Prepare the Waffles:**
   - Preheat your waffle iron according to the manufacturer's instructions.
   - In a large bowl, whisk together the flour, sugar, baking powder, and salt.
   - In another bowl, beat the eggs, then add the milk, melted butter, and vanilla extract. Mix well.
   - Pour the wet ingredients into the dry ingredients and stir until just combined. The batter will be slightly lumpy, which is fine.
   - Cook the waffles in your preheated waffle iron according to the manufacturer's instructions until they are golden brown and crispy.

4. **Assemble the Dish:**
   - Place a waffle on each plate. Top with a piece of fried chicken.
   - Drizzle with maple syrup and a pat of butter if desired. You can also add a dash of hot sauce to the chicken if you like a bit of heat.

5. **Serve:**
   - Serve immediately while the waffles are warm and crispy.

Enjoy your Chicken and Waffles! This dish is perfect for brunch or a comforting meal any time of day.

Stuffed Bell Peppers

Ingredients:

- **4 large bell peppers** (any color: red, green, yellow, or orange)
- **1 lb ground beef** (or ground turkey/chicken for a lighter option)
- **1 small onion**, finely chopped
- **2 cloves garlic**, minced
- **1 cup cooked rice** (white, brown, or wild rice)
- **1 cup tomato sauce** (or diced tomatoes)
- **1 cup shredded cheese** (cheddar, mozzarella, or a mix)
- **1 teaspoon dried oregano**
- **1 teaspoon dried basil**
- **1/2 teaspoon paprika**
- **Salt and pepper**, to taste
- **1 tablespoon olive oil** (for cooking)
- **Fresh parsley** (optional, for garnish)

Instructions:

1. **Preheat the Oven:**
   - Preheat your oven to 375°F (190°C).
2. **Prepare the Bell Peppers:**
   - Cut the tops off the bell peppers and remove the seeds and membranes. If needed, trim the bottom of each pepper slightly so they can stand upright in the baking dish.
   - Blanch the peppers (optional): Boil a pot of water, and cook the peppers for 3-4 minutes until slightly tender. This step helps them cook evenly and retain their shape.
3. **Cook the Filling:**
   - In a large skillet, heat the olive oil over medium heat. Add the chopped onion and cook until softened, about 3-4 minutes.
   - Add the minced garlic and cook for another 30 seconds.
   - Add the ground beef to the skillet and cook until browned, breaking it up with a spoon as it cooks. Drain any excess fat.
   - Stir in the cooked rice, tomato sauce, oregano, basil, paprika, salt, and pepper. Cook for 2-3 minutes until everything is well combined and heated through.
4. **Stuff the Peppers:**
   - Spoon the filling mixture into each bell pepper, packing it in slightly. Place the stuffed peppers upright in a baking dish.
   - Sprinkle shredded cheese on top of each stuffed pepper.
5. **Bake the Peppers:**

- Cover the baking dish with aluminum foil and bake in the preheated oven for 30 minutes.
- Remove the foil and bake for an additional 10-15 minutes, or until the peppers are tender and the cheese is melted and bubbly.

6. **Serve:**
   - Garnish with chopped fresh parsley if desired. Serve the stuffed peppers hot.

Variations:

- **Vegetarian:** Replace the ground beef with cooked lentils, mushrooms, or a mixture of sautéed vegetables.
- **Mexican Style:** Add black beans, corn, and a sprinkle of taco seasoning to the filling. Top with shredded Mexican cheese blend.
- **Mediterranean Style:** Use feta cheese, olives, and chopped tomatoes in the filling, and season with herbs like oregano and dill.

Enjoy your stuffed bell peppers! They're great on their own or served with a simple salad or crusty bread.

Bacon and Egg Breakfast Sandwich

Ingredients:

- **2 slices of bread** (such as English muffin, ciabatta, or sourdough; or use a bagel or croissant for a different twist)
- **2 large eggs**
- **4 strips of bacon**
- **1 slice of cheese** (cheddar, American, Swiss, or your favorite)
- **1 tablespoon butter** (for toasting the bread)
- **Salt and pepper**, to taste
- **Optional:**
    - **Sliced avocado** or **tomato**
    - **Leafy greens** (such as spinach or arugula)
    - **Hot sauce** or **ketchup** for extra flavor

Instructions:

1. **Cook the Bacon:**
    - Heat a skillet over medium heat. Add the bacon strips and cook until crispy, turning occasionally. This should take about 5-7 minutes.
    - Remove the bacon from the skillet and drain on paper towels. Discard some of the excess fat if necessary, but leave a bit in the pan for cooking the eggs.
2. **Toast the Bread:**
    - While the bacon is cooking, spread butter on one side of each bread slice.
    - In a separate skillet, toast the bread slices butter-side down over medium heat until golden brown and crispy. You can also toast the bread in a toaster or toaster oven.
3. **Cook the Eggs:**
    - In the same skillet used for bacon (or a clean one if preferred), crack the eggs into the pan. You can cook them to your desired doneness—sunny-side up, over-easy, or scrambled.
    - Season with salt and pepper to taste. If using cheese, place a slice of cheese on top of the eggs during the last minute of cooking to melt it slightly.
4. **Assemble the Sandwich:**
    - Place one slice of toasted bread on a plate. Layer with bacon strips, followed by the cooked egg (or eggs, if using more).
    - Add any additional toppings like avocado slices, tomato, or leafy greens.
    - Top with the second slice of toasted bread.
5. **Serve:**
    - Cut the sandwich in half if desired and serve immediately while hot.

Feel free to customize your sandwich with your favorite ingredients or add a side of fresh fruit or hash browns for a more complete breakfast. Enjoy your Bacon and Egg Breakfast Sandwich!

Turkey Club Wrap

Ingredients:

- **1 large tortilla** (flour or whole wheat)
- **4-6 slices of turkey breast** (deli-style or roasted)
- **3 slices of bacon**, cooked until crispy
- **2-3 slices of tomato**
- **1/2 avocado**, sliced (optional)
- **1 cup lettuce** (such as romaine or iceberg)
- **2 tablespoons mayonnaise** (or use a blend of mayo and mustard for extra flavor)
- **1 slice of Swiss or cheddar cheese** (optional)

Instructions:

1. **Prepare the Ingredients:**
   - Cook the bacon until crispy, then drain on paper towels.
   - Slice the tomato and avocado if using.
2. **Assemble the Wrap:**
   - Spread the mayonnaise evenly over the tortilla.
   - Layer the turkey slices in the center of the tortilla.
   - Place the crispy bacon on top of the turkey.
   - Add the tomato slices and avocado slices if using.
   - Top with lettuce.
   - If using cheese, place a slice on top of the lettuce.
3. **Wrap It Up:**
   - Fold in the sides of the tortilla, then roll it up from the bottom to enclose the filling.
   - Slice the wrap in half diagonally if desired.
4. **Serve:**
   - Serve immediately, or wrap in parchment paper or foil for a portable meal.

Variations:

- **Add Pickles:** For extra crunch and tang, add sliced pickles to the wrap.
- **Swap Ingredients:** Use chicken breast, ham, or a vegetarian option like grilled vegetables or hummus.
- **Spicy Kick:** Add a few dashes of hot sauce or a spicy mustard for an extra kick.

Enjoy your Turkey Club Wrap! It's a versatile and tasty option that's perfect for a quick meal or a packed lunch.

Shrimp Po' Boy

Ingredients:

For the Shrimp:

- **1 lb large shrimp**, peeled and deveined
- **1 cup buttermilk**
- **1 cup all-purpose flour**
- **1/2 cup cornmeal**
- **1 tablespoon paprika**
- **1 teaspoon garlic powder**
- **1 teaspoon onion powder**
- **1/2 teaspoon cayenne pepper** (optional, for heat)
- **1/2 teaspoon salt**
- **1/4 teaspoon black pepper**
- **Vegetable oil** (for frying)

For the Remoulade Sauce:

- **1/2 cup mayonnaise**
- **2 tablespoons Dijon mustard**
- **1 tablespoon lemon juice**
- **1 tablespoon hot sauce** (adjust to taste)
- **1 tablespoon chopped fresh parsley**
- **1 teaspoon smoked paprika**
- **1/2 teaspoon garlic powder**
- **1/4 teaspoon cayenne pepper** (optional, for heat)
- **Salt and pepper**, to taste

For Assembling the Sandwich:

- **4 French baguettes** or sub rolls
- **1 cup shredded lettuce**
- **1-2 tomatoes**, sliced
- **Pickles** (optional, for garnish)

Instructions:

1. **Prepare the Shrimp:**
   - Place the shrimp in a bowl and pour the buttermilk over them. Let them marinate for about 15-20 minutes.
2. **Prepare the Coating:**

- In a shallow dish, combine the flour, cornmeal, paprika, garlic powder, onion powder, cayenne pepper, salt, and black pepper.
3. **Fry the Shrimp:**
    - Heat about 1-2 inches of vegetable oil in a large skillet or deep fryer to 350°F (175°C).
    - Remove the shrimp from the buttermilk, allowing excess to drip off. Dredge each shrimp in the flour mixture, coating evenly.
    - Fry the shrimp in batches, being careful not to overcrowd, for about 2-3 minutes per side, or until golden brown and cooked through. Remove with a slotted spoon and drain on paper towels.
4. **Make the Remoulade Sauce:**
    - In a bowl, mix together the mayonnaise, Dijon mustard, lemon juice, hot sauce, chopped parsley, smoked paprika, garlic powder, cayenne pepper (if using), salt, and pepper. Adjust seasoning to taste.
5. **Assemble the Sandwiches:**
    - Split the French baguettes or sub rolls lengthwise, but don't cut all the way through.
    - Spread a generous amount of remoulade sauce on both sides of the bread.
    - Layer with shredded lettuce, tomato slices, and fried shrimp.
    - Add pickles if desired.
6. **Serve:**
    - Serve the Po' Boys immediately while the shrimp are crispy and the bread is fresh.

Enjoy your Shrimp Po' Boy! It's a delightful blend of textures and flavors that bring a taste of New Orleans right to your table.

Spinach and Artichoke Dip

Ingredients:

- **1 tablespoon olive oil**
- **2 cloves garlic**, minced
- **1 cup chopped fresh spinach** (or about 1/2 cup frozen spinach, thawed and drained)
- **1 can (14 oz) artichoke hearts**, drained and chopped
- **1/2 cup sour cream**
- **1/2 cup mayonnaise**
- **1 cup grated Parmesan cheese**
- **1 cup shredded mozzarella cheese**
- **1/2 teaspoon salt**
- **1/4 teaspoon black pepper**
- **1/4 teaspoon crushed red pepper flakes** (optional, for a bit of heat)

Instructions:

1. **Preheat the Oven:**
    - Preheat your oven to 375°F (190°C).
2. **Prepare the Base:**
    - In a medium skillet, heat the olive oil over medium heat.
    - Add the minced garlic and cook for about 1 minute, or until fragrant. Be careful not to burn the garlic.
3. **Combine Ingredients:**
    - Add the chopped spinach to the skillet and cook for 2-3 minutes until wilted and any excess moisture has evaporated.
    - Stir in the chopped artichoke hearts and cook for another 2 minutes.
4. **Mix the Dip:**
    - In a medium bowl, combine the sour cream, mayonnaise, grated Parmesan cheese, and shredded mozzarella cheese.
    - Add the cooked spinach and artichokes mixture to the bowl. Stir well to combine.
    - Season with salt, black pepper, and crushed red pepper flakes (if using).
5. **Bake the Dip:**
    - Transfer the mixture to an oven-safe dish or baking dish (a 9-inch pie dish or similar works well).
    - Bake in the preheated oven for 20-25 minutes, or until the dip is bubbly and the top is golden brown.
6. **Serve:**
    - Serve hot with your choice of dippers. Some popular options include:
        - **Tortilla chips**
        - **Pita chips**

- **Fresh vegetables** (carrot sticks, celery, bell pepper slices)
- **Crackers** or **baguette slices**

Variations:

- **Add Protein:** For a heartier dip, you can add cooked chicken or bacon bits.
- **Spice it Up:** Add a dash of hot sauce or a sprinkle of cayenne pepper for extra heat.
- **Herbs:** Mix in fresh herbs like dill or basil for added flavor.

Enjoy your Spinach and Artichoke Dip! It's a creamy, cheesy delight that's sure to be a hit with everyone.

BBQ Brisket Tacos

Ingredients:

For the BBQ Brisket:

- **2 lbs beef brisket**
- **1 tablespoon olive oil**
- **1 tablespoon smoked paprika**
- **1 tablespoon brown sugar**
- **1 tablespoon chili powder**
- **1 teaspoon garlic powder**
- **1 teaspoon onion powder**
- **1 teaspoon cumin**
- **1/2 teaspoon salt**
- **1/2 teaspoon black pepper**
- **1 cup BBQ sauce** (store-bought or homemade)
- **1/2 cup beef broth** (or water)

For the Tacos:

- **8 small corn or flour tortillas**
- **1 cup shredded lettuce**
- **1 cup diced tomatoes**
- **1/2 cup sliced red onions** (pickled or fresh)
- **1/2 cup chopped fresh cilantro**
- **1/2 cup crumbled queso fresco** or shredded cheese
- **Lime wedges**, for serving

Instructions:

1. **Prepare the Brisket:**
    - Preheat your oven to 300°F (150°C).
    - In a small bowl, mix together the smoked paprika, brown sugar, chili powder, garlic powder, onion powder, cumin, salt, and black pepper.
    - Rub the spice mixture all over the brisket.
    - Heat the olive oil in a large oven-safe pot or Dutch oven over medium-high heat. Sear the brisket on all sides until browned, about 2-3 minutes per side.
    - Remove the brisket from the pot and set aside.
    - Add the beef broth to the pot, scraping up any browned bits from the bottom.
    - Return the brisket to the pot and cover with BBQ sauce.
    - Cover the pot with a lid and transfer it to the preheated oven. Bake for 3-4 hours, or until the brisket is tender and easily shredded with a fork.
2. **Shred the Brisket:**
    - Remove the brisket from the oven and let it rest for 10-15 minutes.
    - Transfer the brisket to a cutting board and shred it using two forks. Return the shredded brisket to the pot with the BBQ sauce and stir to combine.

3. **Prepare the Tacos:**
    - Warm the tortillas in a dry skillet over medium heat or wrap them in a damp paper towel and microwave for about 30 seconds until soft and pliable.
    - Spoon the shredded BBQ brisket onto the tortillas.
4. **Top the Tacos:**
    - Top each taco with shredded lettuce, diced tomatoes, sliced red onions, and crumbled queso fresco.
    - Garnish with fresh cilantro.
5. **Serve:**
    - Serve the BBQ Brisket Tacos with lime wedges on the side for squeezing over the top.

Optional Additions:

- **Pickled Jalapeños:** For a spicy kick.
- **Avocado Slices:** For added creaminess.
- **Sour Cream or Greek Yogurt:** For a tangy touch.

Enjoy your BBQ Brisket Tacos! They're a perfect blend of smoky, savory brisket and fresh, zesty taco toppings.

Veggie Frittata

Ingredients:

- **1 tablespoon olive oil**
- **1 small onion**, diced
- **1 bell pepper**, diced (any color)
- **1 cup broccoli florets** (or other veggies like spinach, zucchini, or mushrooms)
- **1 cup cherry tomatoes**, halved (optional)
- **6 large eggs**
- **1/2 cup milk** (whole or 2% for creaminess; can use dairy-free milk if preferred)
- **1 cup shredded cheese** (such as cheddar, mozzarella, or feta)
- **Salt and pepper**, to taste
- **1/2 teaspoon dried oregano** or **thyme** (optional)
- **Fresh herbs** (such as parsley or basil), chopped, for garnish (optional)

Instructions:

1. **Preheat the Oven:**
   - Preheat your oven to 375°F (190°C).
2. **Prepare the Vegetables:**
   - In a large oven-safe skillet (such as a cast-iron skillet), heat the olive oil over medium heat.
   - Add the diced onion and bell pepper. Sauté for about 3-4 minutes, or until they begin to soften.
   - Add the broccoli (and any other vegetables you're using) and cook for another 3-4 minutes until the vegetables are tender. Add the cherry tomatoes if using and cook for an additional 1-2 minutes.
3. **Prepare the Egg Mixture:**
   - In a medium bowl, whisk together the eggs, milk, salt, pepper, and dried oregano or thyme.
4. **Combine and Cook:**
   - Pour the egg mixture over the sautéed vegetables in the skillet, making sure to evenly distribute the eggs.
   - Sprinkle the shredded cheese evenly over the top.
5. **Bake the Frittata:**
   - Transfer the skillet to the preheated oven and bake for 20-25 minutes, or until the frittata is set and the top is golden brown. You can test doneness by inserting a knife in the center; it should come out clean.
6. **Serve:**
   - Allow the frittata to cool slightly before slicing.
   - Garnish with fresh herbs if desired.

Variations:

- **Add Protein:** Incorporate cooked bacon, sausage, or ham for extra protein.
- **Different Veggies:** Use whatever vegetables you have on hand, such as asparagus, mushrooms, or spinach.
- **Cheese Options:** Experiment with different cheeses like goat cheese, Gruyère, or Parmesan.

Tips:

- **Make Ahead:** Frittatas can be made ahead of time and stored in the refrigerator for up to 4 days. They also freeze well for up to 3 months.
- **Serving Suggestions:** Pair with a side salad, fresh fruit, or whole-grain toast for a complete meal.

Enjoy your Veggie Frittata! It's a delicious and flexible dish that can be tailored to suit your tastes and what you have on hand.

Beef and Cheddar Sliders

Ingredients:

For the Sliders:

- **1 lb ground beef**
- **1/2 teaspoon salt**
- **1/4 teaspoon black pepper**
- **1/2 teaspoon garlic powder**
- **1/2 teaspoon onion powder**
- **8-12 slider buns** (or mini rolls)
- **4 slices cheddar cheese**, cut into smaller pieces to fit the sliders
- **Butter** (for brushing the buns)

For the Slider Topping (optional):

- **2 tablespoons butter**, melted
- **1 tablespoon Dijon mustard**
- **1 tablespoon Worcestershire sauce**
- **1 tablespoon brown sugar**
- **1/2 teaspoon poppy seeds** (optional)
- **1/2 teaspoon sesame seeds** (optional)
- **1/2 teaspoon dried onion flakes** (optional)

Instructions:

1. **Prepare the Beef Patties:**
   - In a mixing bowl, combine the ground beef with salt, black pepper, garlic powder, and onion powder. Mix until just combined.
   - Form the mixture into 8-12 small patties, depending on the size of your slider buns.
2. **Cook the Beef Patties:**
   - Heat a skillet or grill over medium-high heat.
   - Cook the patties for about 3-4 minutes per side, or until they reach an internal temperature of 160°F (71°C) for medium doneness.
   - During the last minute of cooking, place a piece of cheddar cheese on each patty and cover with a lid to melt the cheese.
3. **Prepare the Slider Buns:**
   - Preheat your oven to 375°F (190°C).
   - Brush the cut sides of the slider buns with melted butter.
   - Place the buns on a baking sheet and bake for 5-7 minutes, or until they are lightly toasted.

4. **Assemble the Sliders:**
   - Place the cooked beef patties with melted cheese on the bottom half of each slider bun.
   - Top with the other half of the bun.
5. **Prepare the Slider Topping (optional):**
   - In a small bowl, mix together the melted butter, Dijon mustard, Worcestershire sauce, and brown sugar.
   - Brush the mixture over the tops of the sliders.
   - Sprinkle with poppy seeds, sesame seeds, and dried onion flakes if using.
6. **Bake the Sliders (optional):**
   - If you added the optional topping, bake the assembled sliders in the oven for an additional 5 minutes to allow the flavors to meld and the sliders to be heated through.
7. **Serve:**
   - Serve the Beef and Cheddar Sliders warm.

Variations:

- **Add Toppings:** Customize your sliders with additional toppings such as pickles, sautéed onions, or lettuce.
- **Sauces:** Offer condiments like ketchup, mustard, or BBQ sauce on the side for extra flavor.

These Beef and Cheddar Sliders are sure to be a hit with family and friends. Enjoy!

Roasted Vegetable Panini

Ingredients:

- **1 large eggplant**, sliced into 1/4-inch rounds
- **1 large zucchini**, sliced into 1/4-inch rounds
- **1 red bell pepper**, sliced
- **1 yellow bell pepper**, sliced
- **1 red onion**, sliced
- **2 tablespoons olive oil**
- **Salt and pepper**, to taste
- **1 teaspoon dried oregano** (or fresh, if available)
- **4 slices of your favorite bread** (such as ciabatta, sourdough, or focaccia)
- **1/2 cup pesto** (store-bought or homemade)
- **4 slices of provolone, mozzarella, or goat cheese**
- **1/4 cup balsamic glaze** (optional, for drizzling)
- **Fresh basil leaves** (optional, for garnish)

Instructions:

1. **Roast the Vegetables:**
   - Preheat your oven to 400°F (200°C).
   - Arrange the sliced eggplant, zucchini, bell peppers, and red onion on a large baking sheet.
   - Drizzle with olive oil and season with salt, pepper, and dried oregano.
   - Toss the vegetables to coat them evenly.
   - Roast in the preheated oven for 20-25 minutes, or until the vegetables are tender and slightly caramelized. Stir halfway through to ensure even roasting.
2. **Prepare the Panini:**
   - Preheat a panini press or grill pan over medium heat.
   - Spread pesto evenly on one side of each bread slice.
   - Layer roasted vegetables and cheese slices on the non-pesto side of two bread slices.
   - Top with the remaining bread slices, pesto side down.
3. **Grill the Panini:**
   - If using a panini press, place the sandwiches in the press and cook according to the manufacturer's instructions, usually about 4-6 minutes, until the bread is crispy and the cheese is melted.
   - If using a grill pan, place the sandwiches in the pan and press down with a heavy object or another pan. Grill for 3-4 minutes per side, or until the bread is golden brown and the cheese is melted. You may need to flip the sandwiches carefully.
4. **Serve:**

- Remove the panini from the press or grill pan.
- If desired, drizzle with balsamic glaze and garnish with fresh basil leaves.

Tips:

- **Customize:** Feel free to add other ingredients like sun-dried tomatoes, olives, or caramelized onions.
- **Make It a Meal:** Serve the panini with a side salad or some crispy kettle chips for a complete meal.

Enjoy your Roasted Vegetable Panini! It's a flavorful, satisfying sandwich that highlights the natural sweetness of the roasted vegetables.

www.ingramcontent.com/pod-product-compliance
Lightning Source LLC
LaVergne TN
LVHW081559060526
838201LV00054B/1971